35657NPBN Bream Treble
Round bend; Fine gauge; Extra strong; Short shank; Size 14 - 10

HPTG76 Elite Vandam Treble
Micro sharp; Wide gap; 30% stronger; 2x short shank; Size 8 - 1

36330NP-DS Saltism Treble
Micro sharp; Durasteel; 2x short shank; 4x strong; Size 6 to 3/0

32368NP-DS Kaiju
Super sharp; Durasteel; 7x strong; Welded eye; Size 3/0 to 7/0

MRSF
Snapper Files Rig

MRLRF
Long Red Flasher Rigs

MRBRF
Big Red Flasher Rigs

MRFWR
Fine Worm 2 Hook Whiting

MRDTFR
Demon Terakihi Flasher Rigs

MRHR Hapuka Rig
Size 12/0 - 16/0; Qty 5 per Pack

MRBCR 2-in-1 Bait Catcher Rigs
Size 4 - 10; Qty 10 per Pack

www.mustad.no | www.facebook.com/mustadasia

Geoff Wilson's
COMPLETE BOOK OF
FISHING™
KNOTS & RIGS

First published in 1990 by
Australian Fishing Network

Australian Fishing Network
PO Box 544, Croydon, VIC 3136
Tel: +61 3 9729 8788   Fax: +61 3 9729 7833
Email: sales@afn.com.au
Website: www.afn.com.au

Cardinal Publishers Group
2402 N. Shadeland Ave, Suite A. Indianapolis IN 46219 - 1137
Voice: (317) 352 8200   Fax: (317) 352 8202
Toll Free: (800) 296 0481   www.cardinalpub.com

Reprinted in 1991, 1992, 1993, 1994, 1995, 1996, 1997,
Jan 1998, Dec 1998, 1999, 2000, Feb 2001, Aug 2001, 2002, 2003,
2004, 2005, 2006
Fully Revised & Updated in 2007. Reprinted 2008, 2009, 2010
Colour Update 2011. This edition 2015.

Copyright © Australian Fishing Network 2011

Australia ISBN 9781 8651 3206 8

Geoff Wilson's COMPLETE BOOK OF FISHING KNOTS & RIGS™

All Diagrams, Artwork & Text
GEOFF WILSON

Editor & Consultant
BILL CLASSON

Design & Production
AUSTRALIAN FISHING NETWORK

CONTENTS

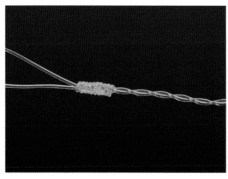

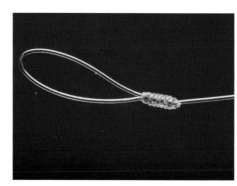

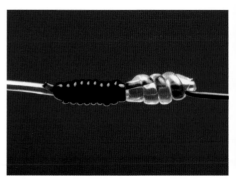

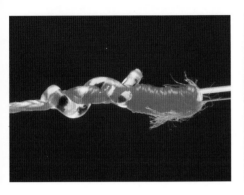
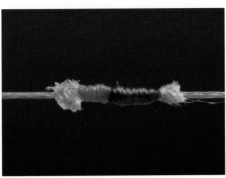
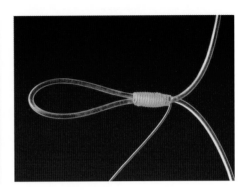

KNOTS
LINE TO TERMINAL TACKLE

LOCKED HALF BLOOD KNOT

This simple and strong knot is adequate for tying hooks and swivels to line testing up to 25 kg breaking strain. It is an especially firm favourite with whiting and snapper anglers.

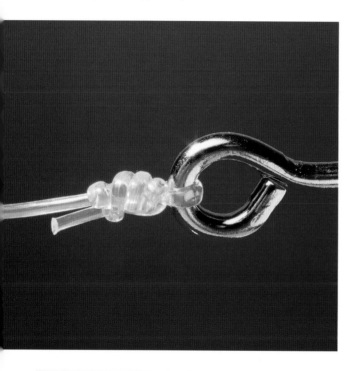

1 Thread the eye of your hook or swivel and twist the tag and main line together.

2 Complete three to six twists and thread the tag back through the first twist. The heavier your line, the less twists you will use.

3 Pull the line so that the knot begins to form. Do not pull it up tight yet or you will have an unlocked half blood which may slip should you be tying new line to a shiny metal surface.

4 To lock the knot, thread the tag through the open loop which has formed at the top of the knot.

5 Pull the knot up firmly and the result should be something like this. Should a loop form within the knot, simply pull on the tag until it disappears.

CLINCH OR BLOOD KNOT
A Geoff Wilson preferred knot

This is undoubtedly the strongest knot for tying a medium size hook to a medium size line such as hook size 4 to 4/0 onto line size 3 kg to 15 kg.

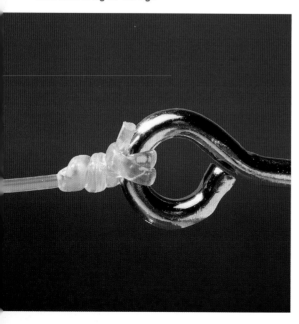

1 Thread the eye of the hook with the line.

2 And make an extra wrap.

3 Then wrap the tag around the main line from three to five times. The heavier the line you are using, the less the number of wraps. The lighter the line, the more wraps you use.

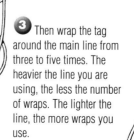

4 Complete the knot by passing the tag back through the first two wraps you made before pulling the knot tight. The best result is achieved when the loops through the eye of the hook retain their wrapping sequence and don't spring apart.

REVERSE TWIST BLOOD KNOT

The following knot illustrates how additional wraps can be made to blood knots by making at least half the wraps required in the usual direction, the rest in the opposite direction.

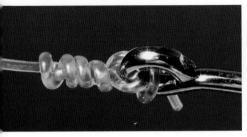

PALOMAR KNOT

The Palomar knot provides a simple means of attaching hooks, either to the end of your line or trace, or along your line as is the case when rigging a drop-shot for soft plastics.

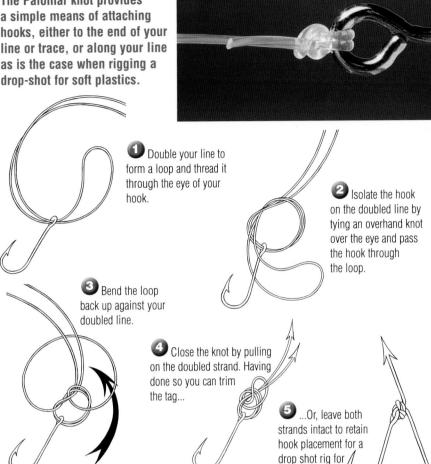

1 First, when tying on a hook, thread line through the eye of the hook.

2 In this case we do an extra wrap to ensure the knot doesn't slip.

3 Twist the tag and standing part of the line together.

4 Do this three times, then wind the tag back in the other direction around the first wraps as shown.

5 Wind the tag back three times and thread it through the centre of the double loop on the eye of the hook so you have three turns up and three turns back. (This is for monofilament. Do six up and six back for gelspun lines but more on those later).

6 Finish the knot with pressure on the standing part against the hook. Some pressure on the tag may be required to take up the slack here as well.

1 Double your line to form a loop and thread it through the eye of your hook.

2 Isolate the hook on the doubled line by tying an overhand knot over the eye and pass the hook through the loop.

3 Bend the loop back up against your doubled line.

4 Close the knot by pulling on the doubled strand. Having done so you can trim the tag...

5 ...Or, leave both strands intact to retain hook placement for a drop shot rig for soft plastics.

GARY MARTIN'S WORLD'S FAIR KNOT

Gary Martin called this knot the 'World's Fair Knot' after being selected the winner from 498 entries in an international, original, fishing knot competition conducted by Du Pont at the Knoxville, USA, World's Fair in 1982. It is quick and easy to tie yet shows no tendency to slip.

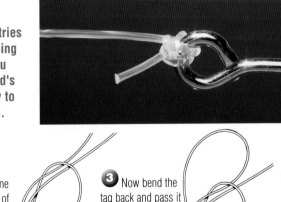

1 Make a loop in your line and pass it through the eye of your hook or swivel.

2 Fold the protruding section of the loop back over the double strand.

3 Now bend the tag back and pass it over the folded loop and under the doubled strand as shown.

4 Now pass the tag through the loop formed by the previous step.

5 Shown is the finished knot formed with gentle but firm pressure on the main line.

CENTAURI KNOT *A Geoff Wilson preferred knot*

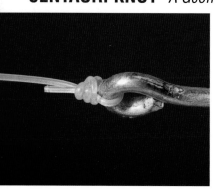

First published by fishing writer Dick Lewers, the Centauri knot is useful over a wide range of line diameters because it forms with a minimum of friction and therefore does not distort the line. Ideal for small hooks, rings and swivels.

1 Thread the eye of hook or swivel with the tag and make the configuration shown, first passing the tag behind the main line. The crossover is held between thumb and index finger of the left hand to facilitate tying.

2 The first step is repeated and the second crossover also held between thumb and index finger of the left hand.

3 Again, the tag is passed behind the main line and the crossover held between thumb and finger. I will point out that some anglers make only two wraps, not three, but this produces a weaker knot.

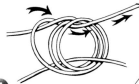

4 Now tuck the tag through the centre of the three loops you have made and form the knot by pulling gently on the tag against the hook or swivel. Ideally the loops should close up evenly.

5 Having formed the knot, the loop will have enlarged. Simply slide the knot down the leader onto the eye of the hook or swivel.

6 The finished knot should lock down onto the eye of the hook with the tag pointing back up the leader.

PITZEN KNOT

Credited to Edgar Pitzenbauer of Germany, the Pitzen knot is useful for tying monofilament to hooks, rings and swivels.

The chief advantage of the Pitzen Knot is that it is very small which makes it a favourite with fly fishermen. It is also very strong when tied correctly.

1 Thread the eye of the hook and loop the tag back under the standing part.

2 Wind the tag back around the loop so another smaller loop is formed at the beginning of the knot.

3 Make three wraps in all then pass the tag back through the small loop as shown.

4 With gentle pressure on the tag, close the knot around the standing part of the line but not too tight; just like I've drawn it here. If you tighten it right up now, the strength of the final knot will be reduced quite a bit.

5 Slide the knot down the standing part, onto eye of the hook and tighten, this time with firm pressure until you feel the knot sort of click into place. Then trim the tag.

MARSHALL'S SNARE

This method of tying on a hook was introduced to anglers by Australian fishing writer Frank Marshall some decades ago. It is simple to tie in the dark and adequately strong for most situations.

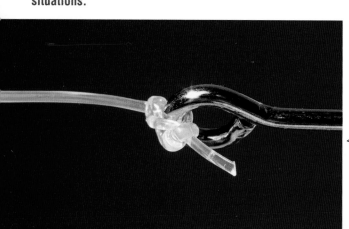

1 First make a loop in the end of your line and tie an overhand knot with the tag, encircling the main line.

2 Pass the loop through the eye of your hook.

3 Pass the loop entirely over the hook and pass the tag through the loop as well.

4 Close the overhand knot and pull the noose up tight around the hook.

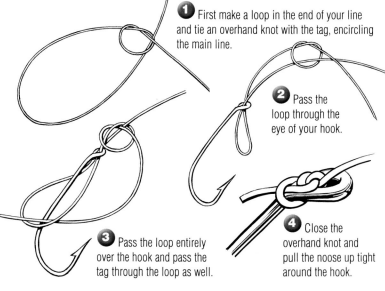
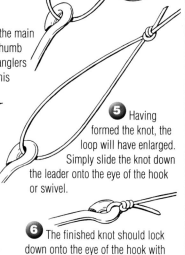

REBECK KNOT

Introduced to anglers by Barry Rebeck of South Africa, the Rebeck knot provides a simple and secure hook connection.

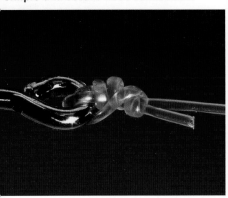

1 Thread the eye of the hook and wrap the leader around the shank.

2 Make four complete wraps and thread the eye of the hook once more.

3 Take a firm hold of the hook in both hands as shown.

4 And slide the wraps that you made on the shank, up and over the eye.

5 At this stage the knot looks like this.

6 Close the knot by pulling gently on the main line, then on the tag to close the second loop.

PENNY KNOT

This excellent method of attaching a hook or fly is named after Ron Penny. This description of the knot, and technique of tying it, is by Peter Hayes of Premier Guides.

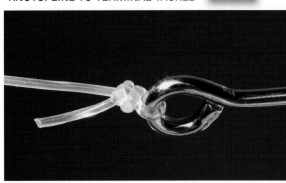

1 Thread the hook, which is held between thumb and third finger of the left hand. The tag, which is extended in a loop, is held between index finger and thumb. The standing part of the line is held in the palm of the right hand and looped over the right index finger as shown.

2 The right index finger, still retaining the loop in the standing part of the line, goes in the loop of the tag.

3 Pulls it back over the standing part, which was looped over the right index finger.

4 And rotates it anti-clockwise around the standing part.

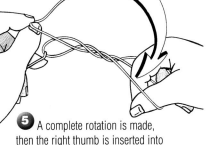

5 A complete rotation is made, then the right thumb is inserted into the loop beside the index finger to grip the tag on completion of another half rotation.

6 The tag is pulled free of the left thumb and finger grip and through the loop as shown.

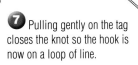

7 Pulling gently on the tag closes the knot so the hook is now on a loop of line.

8 The knot is slid down onto the eye of the hook and locked in place with firm, but gentle pressure, on the standing part of the line. The tag is trimmed short.

UNI KNOT

The Uni Knot is widely used for attaching hooks, rings and swivels to the end of the line.

THUMB KNOT

This knot is used for attaching hooks, rings or swivels to the very heaviest nylon monofilament.

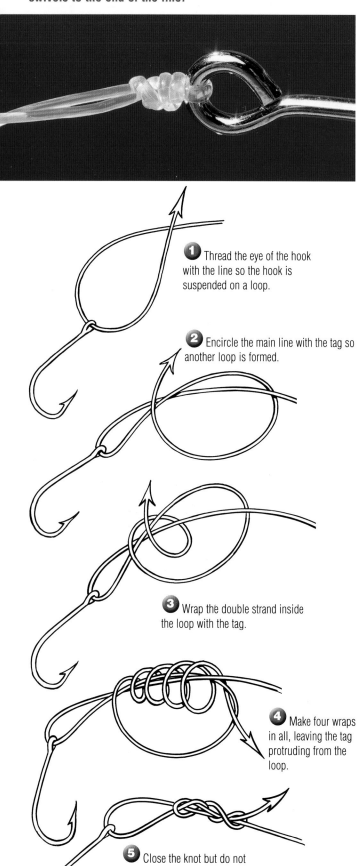

1 Thread the eye of the hook with the line so the hook is suspended on a loop.

2 Encircle the main line with the tag so another loop is formed.

3 Wrap the double strand inside the loop with the tag.

4 Make four wraps in all, leaving the tag protruding from the loop.

5 Close the knot but do not pull it tight just yet.

6 Slide the knot down onto the eye of the hook, pull it tight and trim the tag.

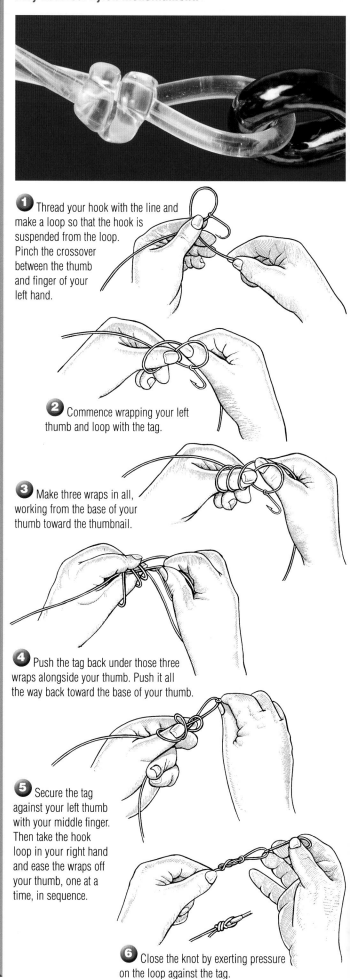

1 Thread your hook with the line and make a loop so that the hook is suspended from the loop. Pinch the crossover between the thumb and finger of your left hand.

2 Commence wrapping your left thumb and loop with the tag.

3 Make three wraps in all, working from the base of your thumb toward the thumbnail.

4 Push the tag back under those three wraps alongside your thumb. Push it all the way back toward the base of your thumb.

5 Secure the tag against your left thumb with your middle finger. Then take the hook loop in your right hand and ease the wraps off your thumb, one at a time, in sequence.

6 Close the knot by exerting pressure on the loop against the tag.

NAIL KNOT WITH LOOP

This knot is used for tying hooks to heavy monofilament leaders because it pulls up without damaging the line.

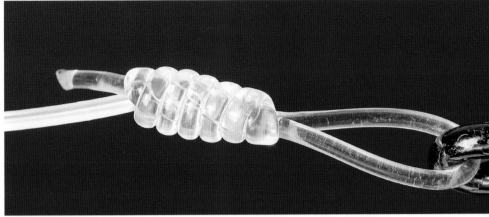

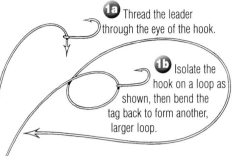

1a Thread the leader through the eye of the hook.

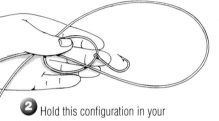

1b Isolate the hook on a loop as shown, then bend the tag back to form another, larger loop.

2 Hold this configuration in your hand as shown.

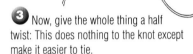

3 Now, give the whole thing a half twist: This does nothing to the knot except make it easier to tie.

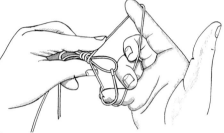

4 Wrap the small loop, from which the hook is suspended, with the larger loop, catching the wraps in sequence with your thumb, index finger, and middle finger of your left hand; the reverse should you be left handed.

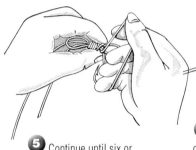

5 Continue until six or seven wraps have been made.

6 At this stage the configuration of the knot would be as shown if unobstructed by the hands.

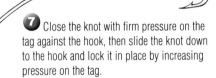

7 Close the knot with firm pressure on the tag against the hook, then slide the knot down to the hook and lock it in place by increasing pressure on the tag.

CAT'S PAW

Having tied a Twisted Double with an End Loop, a wire snap, snap swivel or other metal fitting, may be attached using a Cat's Paw.

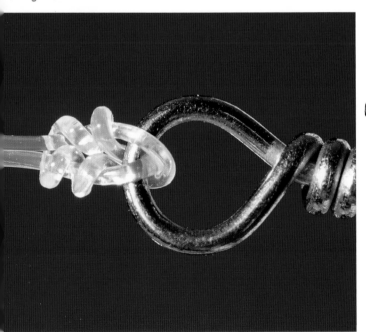

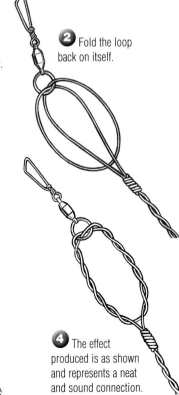

1 Thread the end loop through the eye of the metal fitting, a large snap swivel in this case.

2 Fold the loop back on itself.

3 Rotate the swivel through the loop three times (in either direction).

4 The effect produced is as shown and represents a neat and sound connection.

SNELLS
LINE TO TERMINAL TACKLE

SIMPLE SNELL

This is the first fishing knot I ever learned. My father showed it to me at age five or six. It is a safe and sound way of attaching a hook to a snood but it requires a upturned eye hook like the Mustad 92554, or an downturned eye hook like the Mustad 540 (illustrated) to be effective. It also requires both ends of the snood line to be free because both have to be threaded through the eye of the hook.

After discarding this attachment for many years, I am using it again for tying the hooks onto bait jigs because it provides a particularly quick and satisfactory method of not only attaching the hook, but also facilitating the easy addition of a small piece of wool to the hook to act as a fish attractor.

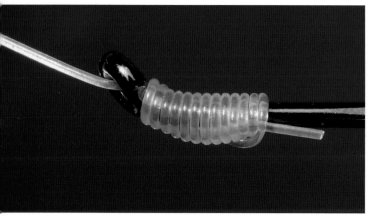

1 Thread the tag end of the snood line through the eye of the hook from underneath and bend it back against the shank of the hook.

2 Wrap both the tag and the shank of the hook with the main line of the snood.

3 Having completed nine or ten wraps, thread the other end of the snood line through the eye of the hook, once again from underneath, and pull the line up tight.

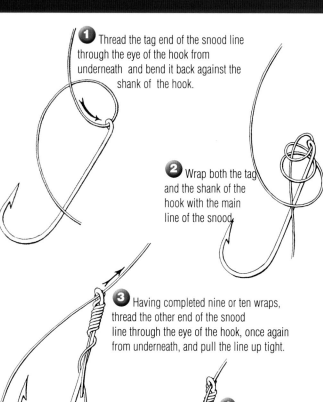

4 Trim the tag to finish the knot and the result should look like this. The main line runs over the wraps, not underneath as in the common snell, avoiding the risk of a separation through the line being cut by a partially open eye.

COMMON SNELL

Originally introduced for hooks with spatulate eyes, the Snell is appropriate for hooks with up or down turned eyes when the leader needs to be aligned along the shank of the hook. This knot is most important in many two-hook rigs. The eye of the hook need not be threaded.

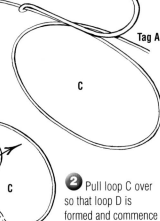

1 Make this configuration in the line against the hook. The eye may be threaded, but it is not always preferred. Indeed, using hooks with spatulate, knobbed or flattened eyes it is impossible.

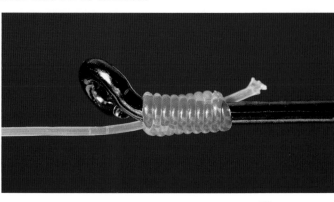

2 Pull loop C over so that loop D is formed and commence wrapping the shank of the hook and the tag.

3 Your snell should begin to look something like this.

4 Continue until the required number of wraps is in place.

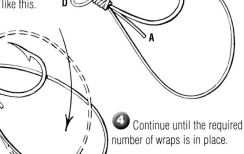

5 Pull on main line B against tag A until the knot is formed on the shank. When the eye of the hook is threaded, it is preferred that the snell is formed down a little from the eye so that the chances of a separation occurring from a roughly turned or sharp eye are reduced.

MULTIPLE HOOK RIGS: SLIDING SNELL

This is the adjustable two-hook rig I use for mulloway. The hooks can be drawn apart or closed up depending on the size of bait being used. It is a bit tricky to make but works well.

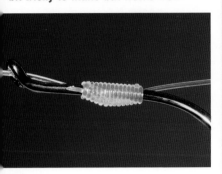

1 Take one hook and a length of line, (separate from, and lighter than, the leader) then make this configuration.

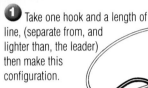

2 Roll the loop around the hook. You will need to do this a number of times.

3 This I how I do it – it's really quite easy provided the tags are not too long.

4 Continue until you have made at least six wraps. I usually do a few more. Then introduce the leader through the eye of the hook.

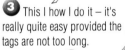

5 Continue to wrap over the leader four or five times so the leader is bound tightly to the hook. Don't use too many wraps, otherwise the hook won't be able to slide without damaging the leader.

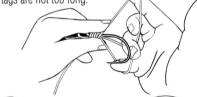

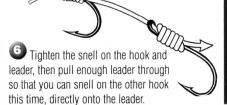

6 Tighten the snell on the hook and leader, then pull enough leader through so that you can snell on the other hook this time, directly onto the leader.

LOOPS

HOMER RHODE LOOP

This is a useful loop for attaching rapid action lures to heavy monofilament leaders.

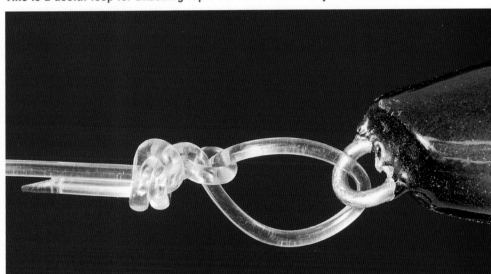

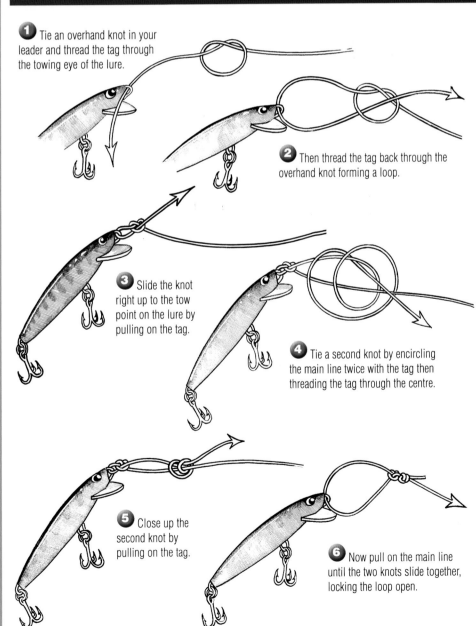

1 Tie an overhand knot in your leader and thread the tag through the towing eye of the lure.

2 Then thread the tag back through the overhand knot forming a loop.

3 Slide the knot right up to the tow point on the lure by pulling on the tag.

4 Tie a second knot by encircling the main line twice with the tag then threading the tag through the centre.

5 Close up the second knot by pulling on the tag.

6 Now pull on the main line until the two knots slide together, locking the loop open.

PERFECTION LOOP

Shown are the steps in attaching a lure to a heavy monofilament leader using the Perfection Loop.

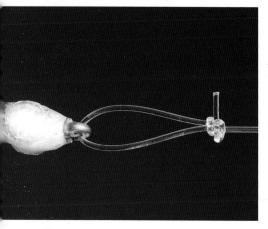

1 Tie an ordinary underhand knot in your leader but don't close it up. Then pass the tag of your leader through the eye of your lure.

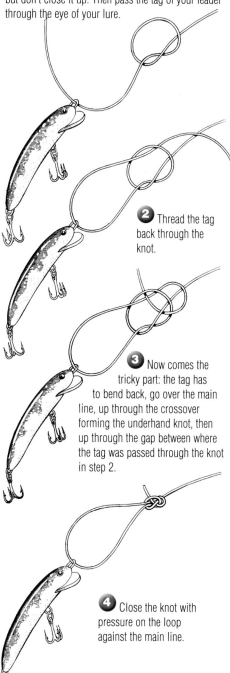

2 Thread the tag back through the knot.

3 Now comes the tricky part: the tag has to bend back, go over the main line, up through the crossover forming the underhand knot, then up through the gap between where the tag was passed through the knot in step 2.

4 Close the knot with pressure on the loop against the main line.

DROPPER LOOP

This loop can be tied anywhere along a length of line for the attachment of a hook or leader.

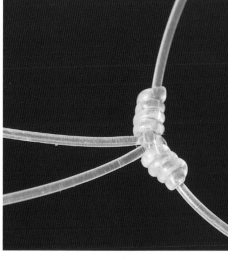

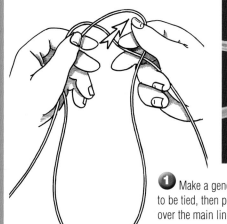

1 Make a generous loop in your line where the dropper is to be tied, then pull out a section of the loop so that it crosses over the main line at one side forming a second smaller loop.

2 Begin twisting the smaller loop, alternating the twisting and holding between hands.

3 Make four complete twists (eight half twists) when using monofilament and six complete twists (twelve half twists) when using gelspun lines. Then thread the larger loop through the smaller loop which you have been twisting.

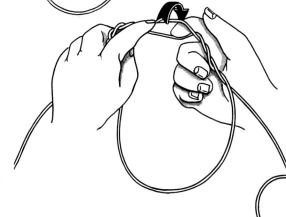

4 Put your larger loop around a peg or the like and gently tension the line both sides of the knot until it pulls up nicely. Particular care needs to be taken with this step when using gelspun or the line can be sheared off at either side of the knot.

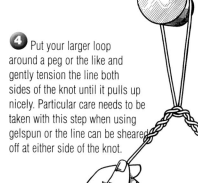

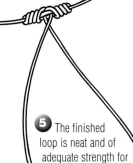

5 The finished loop is neat and of adequate strength for the majority of fishing situations.

TWISTED DROPPER LOOP

Dropper loops facilitate the easy attachment of hooks. Twisting the line before tying a dropper loop stiffens the dropper so that it cannot tangle around the main line

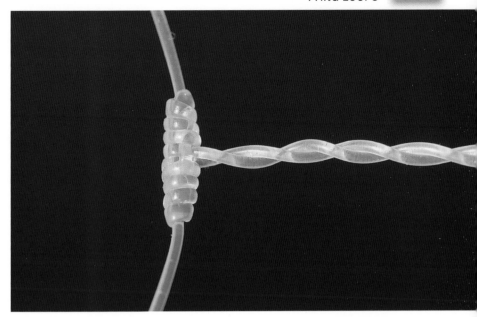

1 Twist the line so a loop spirals out roughly at right angles.

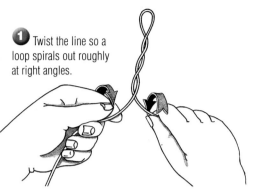

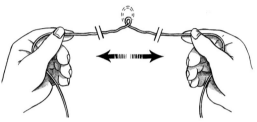

2 Having made a dozen or so twists, twice that number should you be counting the half twists, pull the twisted spiral apart so that:
• One, the loop is reduced to the size where it can be threaded through the eye of a hook.
• Two, the twists are compressed more tightly.

3 Allow the loop to spiral back into place again.

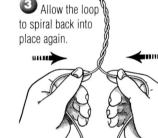

4 Isolate the spiral by crossing the line from each side to form a loop. Your index finger goes between loop and tag.

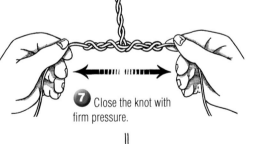

5 Twist the cross-over alternately with each hand, inserting and withdrawing the index finger of each hand as each half twist is made.

6 Having completed four complete twists (eight half twists), pass the spiral through at the cross-over where you were twisting with your fingers.

7 Close the knot with firm pressure.

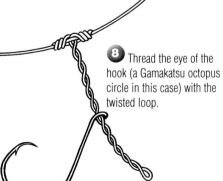

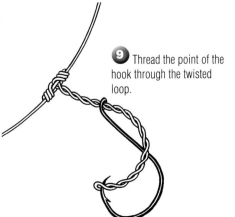

8 Thread the eye of the hook (a Gamakatsu octopus circle in this case) with the twisted loop.

9 Thread the point of the hook through the twisted loop.

10 The hook is presented far enough away from the line so it is most unlikely to tangle.

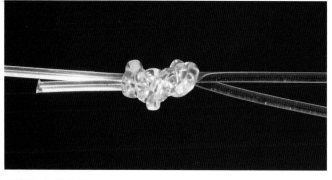

FIGURE OF EIGHT KNOT OR BLOOD BIGHT

Used for loop to loop connections, usually between a short dropper and a dropper loop in the main line.

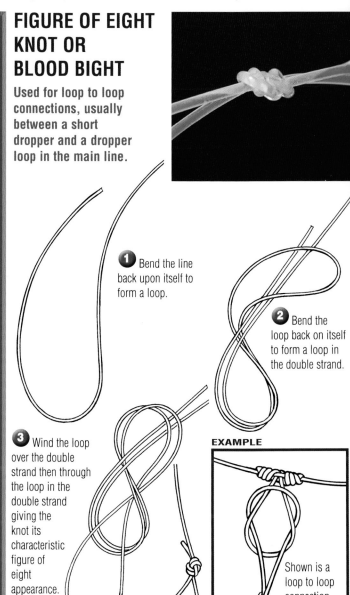

END LOOP

This is one of the quickest and strongest ways of tying an End loop, or Short Double, in monofilament.

1 Make a loop in the end of your mono and wind it back around the doubled strand of tag and main line.

2 Wind it back two or three times. Two for heavy line, three for lighter line.

3 Then wind it back the other way.

4 Make the same number of wraps as you did in the first direction and pass the loop through the loop of doubled line.

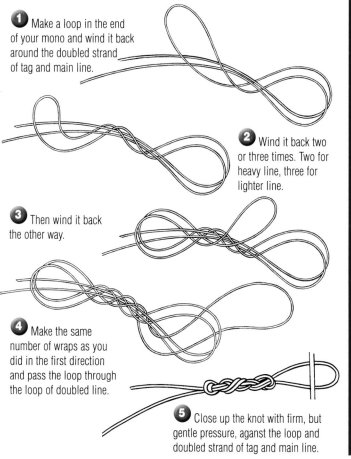

5 Close up the knot with firm, but gentle pressure, agsant the loop and doubled strand of tag and main line.

1 Bend the line back upon itself to form a loop.

2 Bend the loop back on itself to form a loop in the double strand.

3 Wind the loop over the double strand then through the loop in the double strand giving the knot its characteristic figure of eight appearance.

EXAMPLE

Shown is a loop to loop connection with a dropper loop.

4 Close the knot up tight and trim the tag.

DOUBLE OVERHAND LOOP

A quick and easy way to tie a loop on the end of your line.

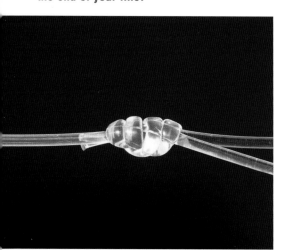

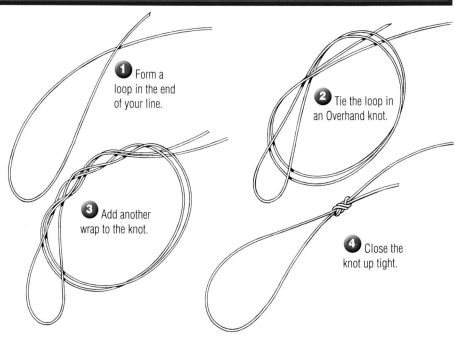

1 Form a loop in the end of your line.

2 Tie the loop in an Overhand knot.

3 Add another wrap to the knot.

4 Close the knot up tight.

KNOTS

RIGGING WITH SUPER LINES

Polyethylene gelspun fishing lines are new, and with these products being improved constantly, there are no absolute rules. However these super lines generally share several properties which include, very high strength for a given diameter and very little stretch; they are also very sheer or slippery. These properties make rigging difficult, but there are knots and rigging strategies for these lines that work very well.

Here we examine some knots and rigging strategies for super lines, but I do point out that my tests on a number of these lines indicated that the breaking strain stated by the manufacturer was usually lower than the actual breaking strain. This could easily give the illusion of very high knot strengths, even with badly chosen or poorly tied knots.

To illustrate my point, I will quote the percentage of manufacturers breaking strain, and probable actual breaking strain, retained by the knots discussed in just two of the several super line products I tested.

One of those products was Berkley Fireline. My tests with 6 and 10 pound Berkley Fireline indicated actual breaking strains of 15 and 25 pounds (6.8 and 11.35 kg) respectively.

Another product was 30 pound Spiderwire (Spectra 2000). Its actual breaking strain was difficult to ascertain but was at least 33 pounds (15 kilograms).

TRIPLE PALOMAR KNOT

The Triple Palomar Knot is recommended for tying super lines to metal rings, towing eyes on lures, and hooks.

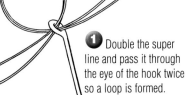

1 Double the super line and pass it through the eye of the hook twice so a loop is formed.

2 Repeat this step twice so three loops of doubled line have been formed on the eye of the hook.

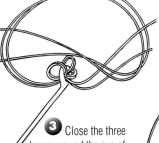

3 Close the three loops around the eye of the hook, then wrap the protruding loop of doubled line back around the mainline and tag. Then pass it back through the loop so an overhand knot is formed.

4 Now, loop the doubled line right over the hook.

5 Close the knot with gentle pressure on mainline and tag, making sure the loop in the doubled line rides up over the eye of the hook and does not bind on the shank below it. Trim the tag.

SILLY SNELL

Although, like the Braid Snell, this very easy hook attachment was unsuitable for use with the finest super lines, it proved suitable for most super lines.

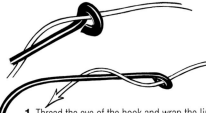

1. Thread the eye of the hook and wrap the line around the shank, taking care you wrap away from the end of the wire which has been rolled to form the eye of the hook: This is most important.

2. Begin wrapping back up the shank of the hook with the tag.

3. Continue almost back to the eye of the hook so that you have a binding some 1.5 cm (5/8") long. Then, simply tuck the tag under the last wrap as shown.

4. Slide the wraps up to the eye of the hook, pulling on the line to tighten the snell.

BRAID SNELL

This knot is suitable for all but the very finest super lines which have a tendency to migrate through the gap between the eye and shank of the hook.

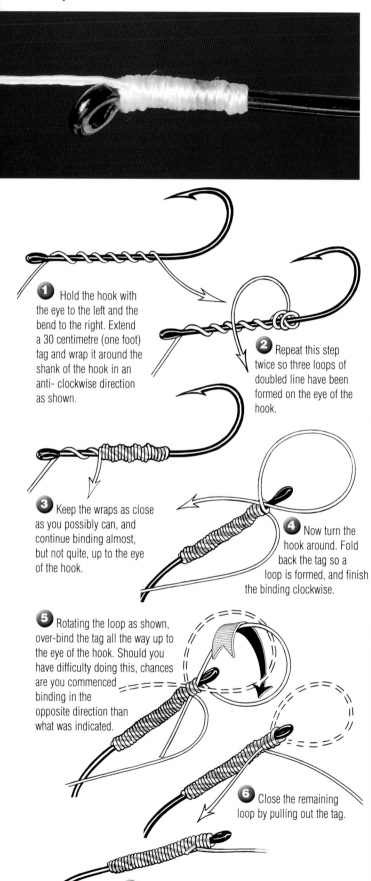

1 Hold the hook with the eye to the left and the bend to the right. Extend a 30 centimetre (one foot) tag and wrap it around the shank of the hook in an anti- clockwise direction as shown.

2 Repeat this step twice so three loops of doubled line have been formed on the eye of the hook.

3 Keep the wraps as close as you possibly can, and continue binding almost, but not quite, up to the eye of the hook.

4 Now turn the hook around. Fold back the tag so a loop is formed, and finish the binding clockwise.

5 Rotating the loop as shown, over-bind the tag all the way up to the eye of the hook. Should you have difficulty doing this, chances are you commenced binding in the opposite direction than what was indicated.

6 Close the remaining loop by pulling out the tag.

7 Shown is the finished snell with the tag trimmed short. The main line emerges from the snell a short distance back from the eye of the hook, although not as far back as it appears to be in this diagram due to the exaggerated thickness of the line.

COLLAR & CAPSTAN

This knot was developed for anglers who prefer tying fine gelspun lines directly to the towing eye of a lure. It tests a good deal higher than most other knots tested.

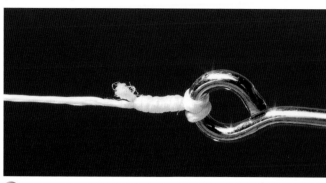

1a First tie a loop in a piece of monofilament of similar breaking strain to the gelspun line. This will be used later as a pull- through to finish the knot.

1b Thread the gelspun line through the towing eye of the lure.

2 Do this at least three times to produce a capstan effect.

3 Introduce the monofilament loop as shown and begin wrapping it with the tag back toward the lure.

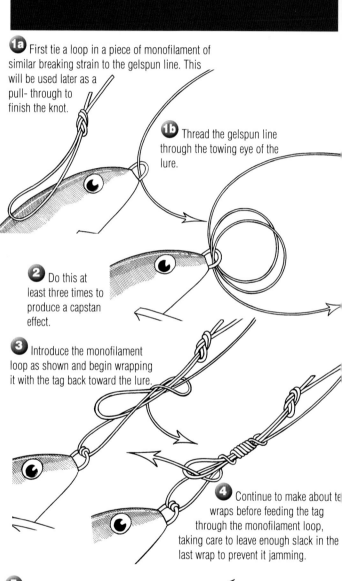

4 Continue to make about te wraps before feeding the tag through the monofilament loop, taking care to leave enough slack in the last wrap to prevent it jamming.

5 Withdraw the mono loop, drawing the tag of the gelspun line back through the knot producing the collar.
  This step is easy enough provided there was some slack in the last wrap of the gelspun line. If there was not, the tag may jam.

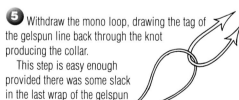

6 Slide the collar (which you have just tied in the tag), down onto the capstan and trim the tag.

BRAID RING KNOT

This is simply a basic blood knot (with two wraps around the eye of the hook in this case) but with quite a few more wraps (or twists) than usual, with the tag and standing part.

We use more wraps in super lines (than with monofilament) to ensure the knot will not slip undone.

1 Pass the line through the hook eye, or ring, twice leaving plenty of tag.

2 Wind the tag around the main line five or six times.

3 Then wind it back again the same number of times.

4 Thread the tag through the centre of both ring wraps.

5 Slide the knot closed with gentle pressure on the main line, stroking the knot back periodically as you do so to keep the wraps in sequence. This prevents them bunching up as the knot closes.

CAT'S PAW SPLICE

This is the highest testing join between two similar diameter gelspun or monofilament lines that I have tested. It requires a loop to be spliced in the end of each line to be joined, preferably using a Bimini Twist, but a Plait would do.

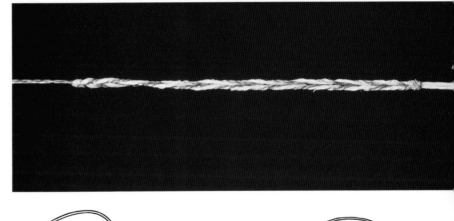

1 Pass the loop in the main line through the loop in the spool of new line, then pass the spool through the loop in the main line.

2 This forms a standard loop to loop connection.

3 Now fold the spool back through the centre of the connection.

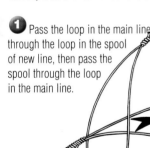

4 Continue to do so until five complete wraps have been made when using monofilament, or ten complete wraps have been made using gelspun line.

5 Spread the series of loops out so they do not tangle, something which may have to be done several times when splicing gelspun lines together.

6 Finally, when the wraps lay in a neat sequence, pull gently on both sides of the splice to produce the effect shown.

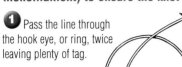

TWISTED LEADER KNOT FOR GELSPUN LINES

This is the strongest method I know of tying a single strand of gelspun line to a monofilament leader.

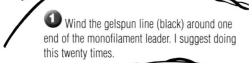

1 Wind the gelspun line (black) around one end of the monofilament leader. I suggest doing this twenty times.

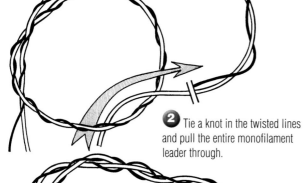

2 Tie a knot in the twisted lines and pull the entire monofilament leader through.

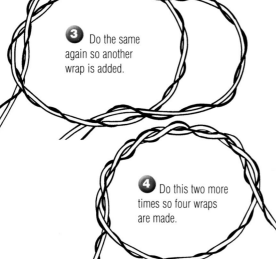

3 Do the same again so another wrap is added.

4 Do this two more times so four wraps are made.

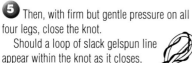

5 Then, with firm but gentle pressure on all four legs, close the knot.
   Should a loop of slack gelspun line appear within the knot as it closes, release the mono leader tag and apply tension to the gelspun line until the loop disappears.

6 Close the knot firmly and trim the tags.

TED DONELAN'S LEADER CONNECTION

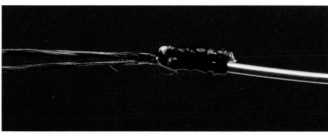

Shown to me by veterinary surgeon and keen angler, Ted Donelan, this superb, streamlined connection between gelspun line and monofilament leader not only retains the lighter line's full strength, but passes easily though the rod guides when either casting or retrieving.

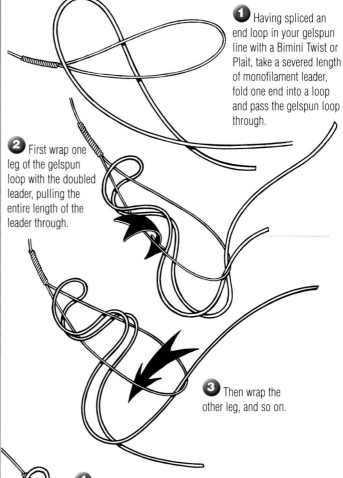

1 Having spliced an end loop in your gelspun line with a Bimini Twist or Plait, take a severed length of monofilament leader, fold one end into a loop and pass the gelspun loop through.

2 First wrap one leg of the gelspun loop with the doubled leader, pulling the entire length of the leader through.

3 Then wrap the other leg, and so on.

4 Continue until four to eight complete wraps are made, the greater the difference in diameter between the two lines, the fewer the number of wraps that are required, and vice versa.

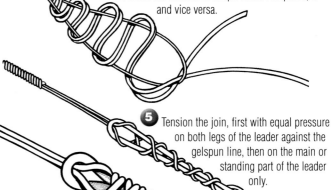

5 Tension the join, first with equal pressure on both legs of the leader against the gelspun line, then on the main or standing part of the leader only.

6 When the join has been pulled up as tight as it will go, cut off the tag.

NAIL KNOT LEADER CONNECTION

This isone of the strongest single-strand connection between a gelspun line and a monofilament leader that I have tested. You will need a slender metal tube or a coarse hypodermic needle like a lumbar puncture to tie it. Open channel nail knots tools will not assist in the tying of this knot.

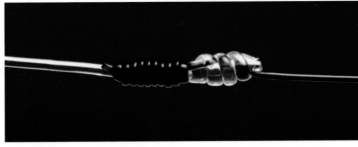

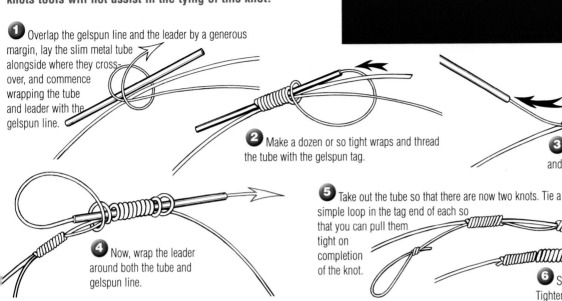

1 Overlap the gelspun line and the leader by a generous margin, lay the slim metal tube alongside where they cross-over, and commence wrapping the tube and leader with the gelspun line.

2 Make a dozen or so tight wraps and thread the tube with the gelspun tag.

3 Slide the tube out and tension the knot.

4 Now, wrap the leader around both the tube and gelspun line.

5 Take out the tube so that there are now two knots. Tie a simple loop in the tag end of each so that you can pull them tight on completion of the knot.

6 Slide the knots together. Tighten each in turn, then trim the tags.

• Please note that although the double nail knot provides a sound connection between gelspun lines and monofilament leaders, it does not offer any advantages when used to join two gelspun lines.

JOINING GELSPUN LINES WITH DOUBLE UNI KNOT

The double Uni Knot has become a firm favourite for joining gelspun lines of similar or different breaking strains. On a good day it will retain 50% of the lighter line's true breaking strain if tied with the additional wraps required.

I specify true breaking strain, because the strength designation on some gelspun lines indicates a much lower breaking strain, sometimes less than half, of what testing indicates.

This fact is responsible for some for some quoting breaking strains as high as 100% for this knot, when controlled testing usually indicates about half that figure.

Some advocate doubling the line before tying this knot. However, unless the doubled line has been secured with a Bimini or other progressive splice to form a secure loop, there is little, if any, advantage in doing so.

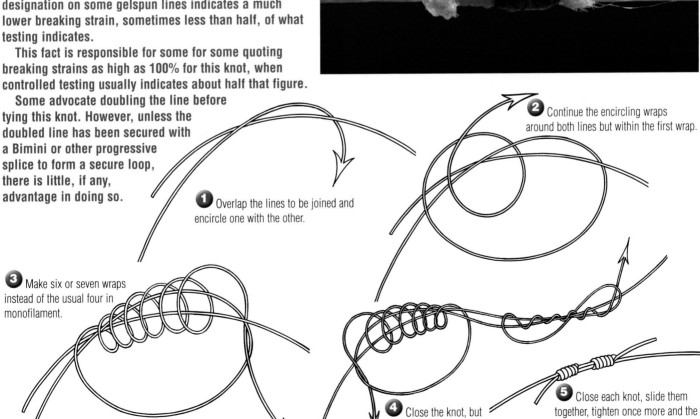

1 Overlap the lines to be joined and encircle one with the other.

2 Continue the encircling wraps around both lines but within the first wrap.

3 Make six or seven wraps instead of the usual four in monofilament.

4 Close the knot, but not tightly; then do the same with the other side.

5 Close each knot, slide them together, tighten once more and the join is complete, all that is required now is to trim the tags.

MIKE CONNOLLY'S LEADER KNOT

Also known as the Stren Knot. A low profile knot that is relatively easy to tie. Tested in three lines, 14 lb Spiderwire Fusion, 30 lb Spiderwire, and 30 lb Fins PRT Braid, this leader knot tested, on average 98.3% of the stated breaking strains of those lines, and 57% of the tested breaking strains.

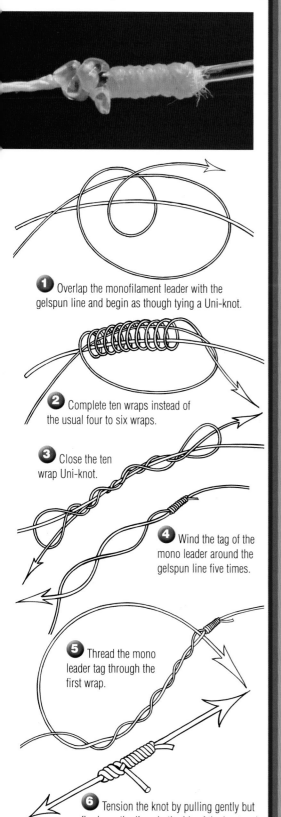

1 Overlap the monofilament leader with the gelspun line and begin as though tying a Uni-knot.

2 Complete ten wraps instead of the usual four to six wraps.

3 Close the ten wrap Uni-knot.

4 Wind the tag of the mono leader around the gelspun line five times.

5 Thread the mono leader tag through the first wrap.

6 Tension the knot by pulling gently but firmly on the lines both side of the knot and trip the tag when the knot has been pulled as tight as it will go.

BRAID LEADER KNOT

The physical properties of gelspun lines suit them admirably to sport, game and deep-sea fishing. However, should you be fishing line class with a view to recording captures under ANSA or IGFA, then it is your responsibility to ensure your line does in fact, test within that designated line class.

For sport, game and deep-sea fishing applications, all terminals are rigged on extended monofilament leaders, which are attached to Bimini doubles tied in the gelspun super line. This is how we add that extended monofilament leader.

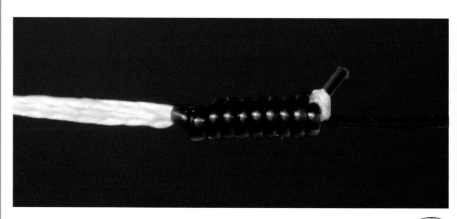

1 Take at least four metres of monofilament, of at least the same, but preferably of a higher breaking strain than that of the gelspun line in which we have just tied a short Bimini Double. Then wind the gelspun loop around one end of your extended monofilament leader.

2 Make at least ten wraps if the breaking strains of the gelspun and the monofilament are similar, but reduce the number of wraps if the monofilament is stronger. Then thread the tag of the monofilament through the loop in the gelspun line.

3 Hold the tag of the monofilament as shown and tension the join so: One, the monofilament tag begins to spiral around the wraps, and Two, the loop in the gelspun line closes.

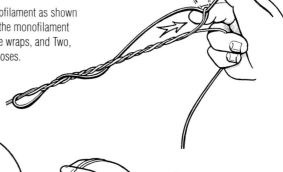

4 Take a firm grip both sides of the join and increase tension until the join closes up. Make sure the join is completely closed before trimming the tag.

CAUTIONARY NOTE While attaching extended monofilament leaders of sufficient length to be wound through the rod guides and onto the reel to gelspun lines, is recommended for the purposes described, it may not be suitable where long casts need to be made. This is because leader knots, travelling through the rod guides at the extremely high speeds associated with long distance casting, may disintegrate after only a few casts.

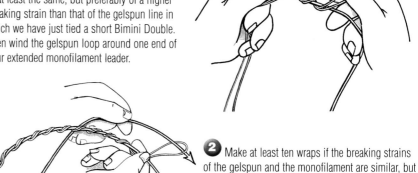

KNOTS

DOUBLE UNI KNOT

Another join worth knowing is the double uni knot, sometimes called a grinner. The double uni-knot is used for joining lines of either similar or different diameters.

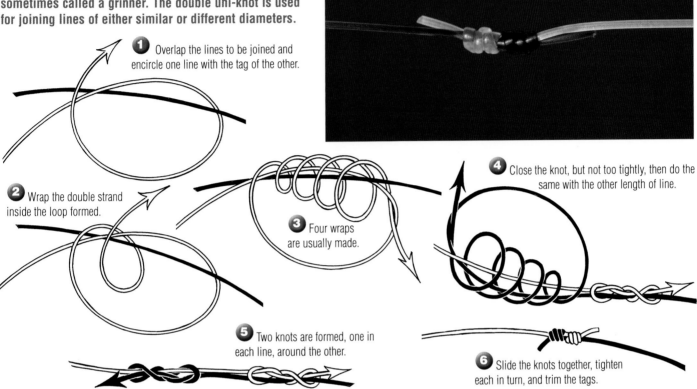

1 Overlap the lines to be joined and encircle one line with the tag of the other.

2 Wrap the double strand inside the loop formed.

3 Four wraps are usually made.

4 Close the knot, but not too tightly, then do the same with the other length of line.

5 Two knots are formed, one in each line, around the other.

6 Slide the knots together, tighten each in turn, and trim the tags.

DOUBLE CENTAURI KNOT FOR JOINING LINES

The Centauri knot was introduced to Australian anglers by fishing writer Dick Lewers as a sound knot for tying on hooks, swivels and rings. However, when two Centauri knots are tied around separate lengths of line, one encircling the other, the join created is strong and durable.

While the best results were obtained when using lines of similar diameter, a satisfactory join could be created in lines of different diameters. Try it and you will be surprised at how strong it is.

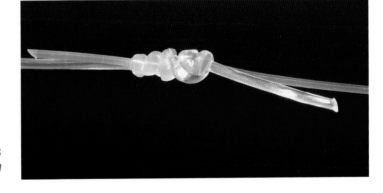

1 Place the two ends to be joined together and encircle one with the other.

2 Make three circles altogether and pass the tag through the middle as shown. Count one and two and three and through.

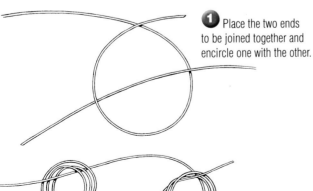

3 Do exactly the same with the opposite number so each length of line encircles the other.

4 Pull each knot up firmly, but not tight.

5 Gently slide both knots together and tighten each in turn. Slide them together once more to close them completely.

DOUBLE FOUR FOLD BLOOD KNOT

Sometimes, we have to join two similar size lines. The Double, Four-Fold Blood knot is widely used because it is neat, easy to tie, and retains adequate strength for most situations.

This knot is useful for joining two lines of the same or similar diameters. It is not satisfactory when there is a significant difference in the diameters of the two lines.

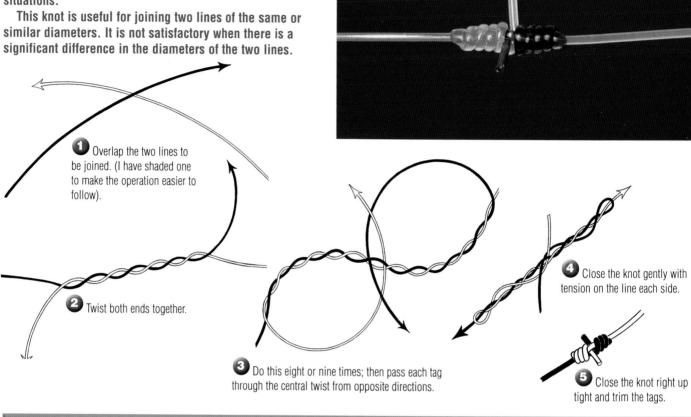

1 Overlap the two lines to be joined. (I have shaded one to make the operation easier to follow).

2 Twist both ends together.

3 Do this eight or nine times; then pass each tag through the central twist from opposite directions.

4 Close the knot gently with tension on the line each side.

5 Close the knot right up tight and trim the tags.

REVERSE TWIST BLOOD KNOT FOR JOINING LINES

The double blood knot requires four wraps each side so it won't slip undone. However, by doubling the wraps each side from four to eight the strength of the knot is substantially increased. We add the four extra wraps each side using the reverse twist principle.

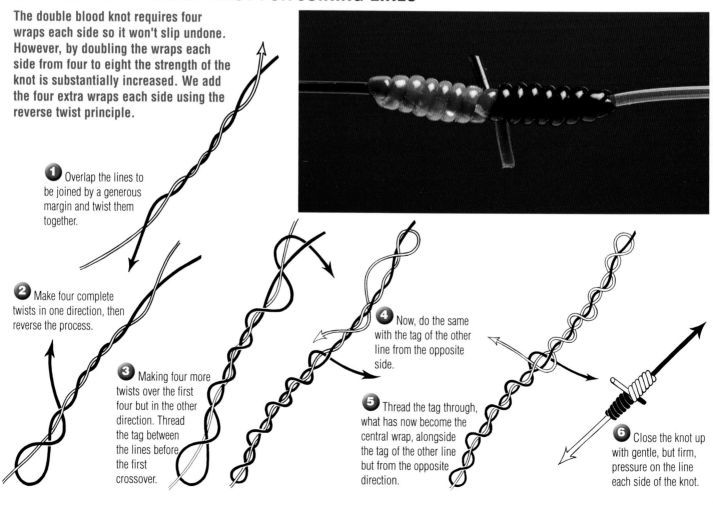

1 Overlap the lines to be joined by a generous margin and twist them together.

2 Make four complete twists in one direction, then reverse the process.

3 Making four more twists over the first four but in the other direction. Thread the tag between the lines before the first crossover.

4 Now, do the same with the tag of the other line from the opposite side.

5 Thread the tag through, what has now become the central wrap, alongside the tag of the other line but from the opposite direction.

6 Close the knot up with gentle, but firm, pressure on the line each side of the knot.

OPPOSED NAIL KNOT

Opposed Nail Knots provide a sound connection between monofilament lines of either the same or different diameters. To tie them you will need a metal tube. Those made by K&S and sold in model aircraft shops are ideal. The smallest tubes, those with an outside diameter of 1/16" and an inside diameter of 1/32" will accommodate lines up to 0.8 mm or 0.3".

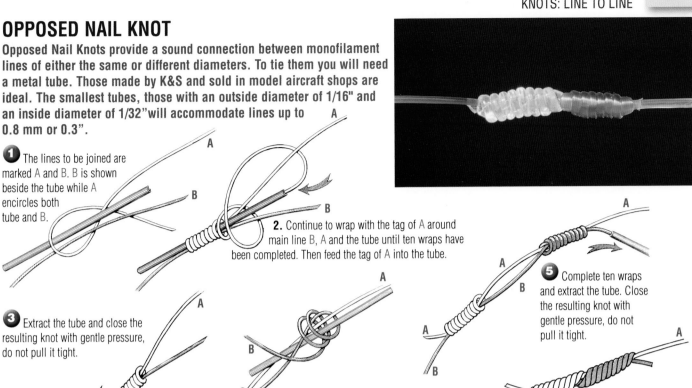

1 The lines to be joined are marked A and B. B is shown beside the tube while A encircles both tube and B.

2. Continue to wrap with the tag of A around main line B, A and the tube until ten wraps have been completed. Then feed the tag of A into the tube.

3 Extract the tube and close the resulting knot with gentle pressure, do not pull it tight.

4 Now lay the tube parallel with line A, extend tag B through the knot and wrap the tube and main lines A and B.

5 Complete ten wraps and extract the tube. Close the resulting knot with gentle pressure, do not pull it tight.

6 Lubricate, pull the knots together, then tighten each in turn. Pull together once more and trim the tags with nail clippers.

PLAITED SPLICE METHOD OF JOINING TWO LINES FOR MAXIMUM STRENGTH.

1 Ideally, line B should be the line coming from the new spool of line, C should be the line coming from your reel. While it is harder to plait like this because the line from the spool is difficult to keep tight, it is better because the leading end of A the plait will go out through the runners first.

This is desirable because the finish of the plait, where the ends are secured, is likely to bunch up if pulled out through the runners under tension. Lay the two ends to be joined as shown.

2 Keeping B tight, pass A over B so that A is now between B and C.

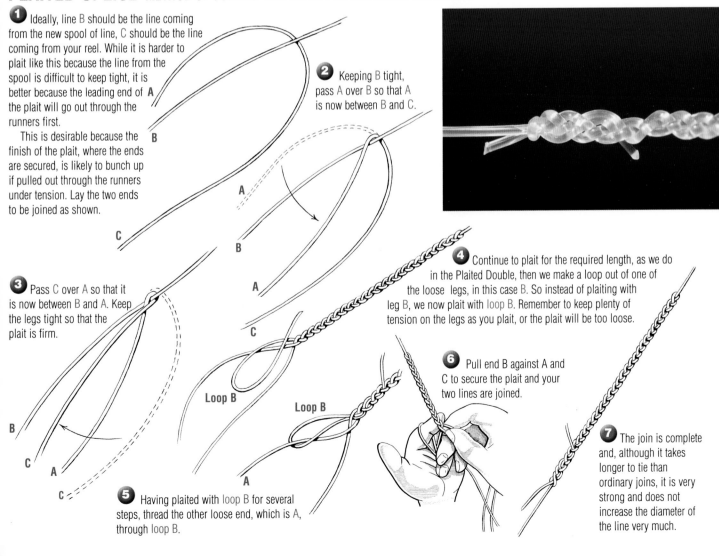

3 Pass C over A so that it is now between B and A. Keep the legs tight so that the plait is firm.

4 Continue to plait for the required length, as we do in the Plaited Double, then we make a loop out of one of the loose legs, in this case B. So instead of plaiting with leg B, we now plait with loop B. Remember to keep plenty of tension on the legs as you plait, or the plait will be too loose.

5 Having plaited with loop B for several steps, thread the other loose end, which is A, through loop B.

6 Pull end B against A and C to secure the plait and your two lines are joined.

7 The join is complete and, although it takes longer to tie than ordinary joins, it is very strong and does not increase the diameter of the line very much.

Loop B

KNOTS

LINE TO LEADER

ALBRIGHT KNOT

Shown is an improved method of tying the Albright Knot.

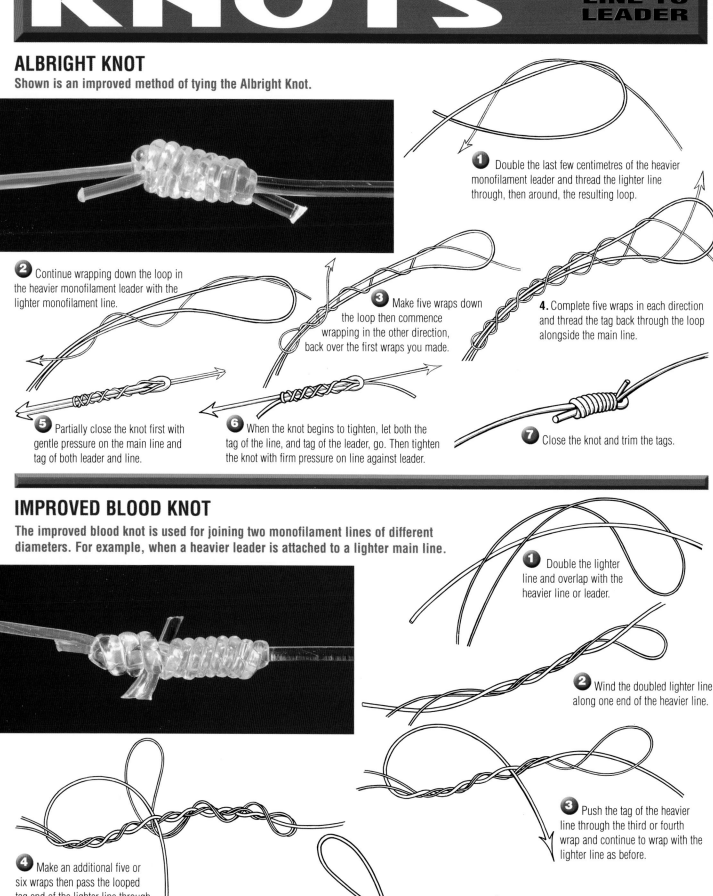

1 Double the last few centimetres of the heavier monofilament leader and thread the lighter line through, then around, the resulting loop.

2 Continue wrapping down the loop in the heavier monofilament leader with the lighter monofilament line.

3 Make five wraps down the loop then commence wrapping in the other direction, back over the first wraps you made.

4. Complete five wraps in each direction and thread the tag back through the loop alongside the main line.

5 Partially close the knot first with gentle pressure on the main line and tag of both leader and line.

6 When the knot begins to tighten, let both the tag of the line, and tag of the leader, go. Then tighten the knot with firm pressure on line against leader.

7 Close the knot and trim the tags.

IMPROVED BLOOD KNOT

The improved blood knot is used for joining two monofilament lines of different diameters. For example, when a heavier leader is attached to a lighter main line.

1 Double the lighter line and overlap with the heavier line or leader.

2 Wind the doubled lighter line along one end of the heavier line.

3 Push the tag of the heavier line through the third or fourth wrap and continue to wrap with the lighter line as before.

4 Make an additional five or six wraps then pass the looped tag end of the lighter line through the same wrap as you passed the tag of the heavier line through. As you can see, I have made five wraps; three up, and two back, before threading with the looped tag end of the lighter line.

5 Close the knot with firm but gentle pressure on the line each side of the knot, taking particular care that no loops of slack line appear in the doubled strand.

6 When the knot has been pulled up really tight, trim the tags.

SLIM BEAUTY

Slim Beauty is a knot used to connect a monofilament main line to a heavier monofilament leader. These are the steps as demonstrated by prominent Australia angler and fishing writer Dean Butler.

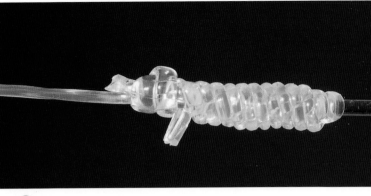

1 Tie a double overhand knot in the heavy monofilament leader.

2 Close the knot until it shows this figure of eight configuration.

3 Make a loop in the end of the monofilament main line and thread it through the figure of eight configuration as shown.

4 Wind the monofilament loop down the heavier leader four times, then wind it back again.

5 Having made four wraps down and four wraps back, thread the remaining monofilament loop between the leader and the descending double strand.

6 Tension the knot by pulling gently, but firmly, on both strands of the monofilament main line, against the heavier monofilament leader. Trim the tags and the join is complete.

TONY JONES' LEADER KNOT

I call this Tony Jones' Leader Knot because I learned it from Captain Tony Jones of Ra Charters.

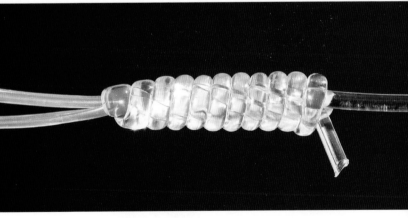

1 Wind your double around the end of your heavy monofilament leader.

2 Make half a dozen wraps or so, but use more wraps for light leaders and less wraps for very heavy leaders.

3 The wind the tag of the leader back around the knot and thread it through the loop in the double.

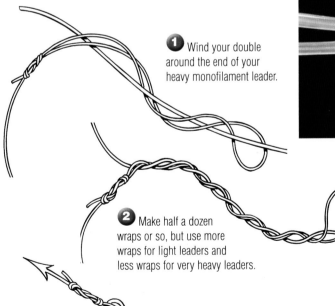
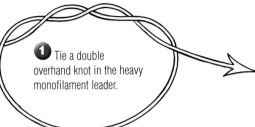

4 Close the leader knot with pressure on the leader against the main line.

5 The finished should join allow the heavy monofilament leader to be wound onto your reel.

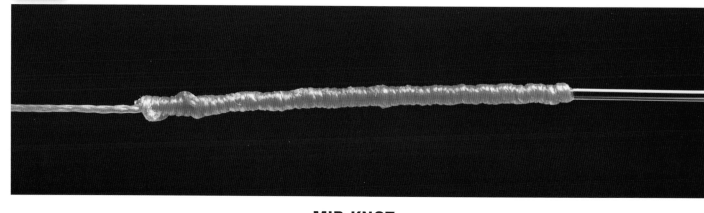

MID KNOT

The term Mid Knot is used to describe a connection between a light line and a heavier leader. It is used mainly for connecting a monofilament leader (either nylon or fluorocarbon) to a gelspun main line.

1 Take a length of monofilament you intend to use as a leader, be it a metre in length or ten metres, and tie a loop in each end.

2 Now, to perform this join to maximum potential, stretch the monofilament leader out between two fixed points so that it is really tight.

3 At one end, commence winding your lighter gelspun line around the stretched leader in a spiral fashion.

4 Extend the spiral for a dozen or so wraps, then over-bind the spiral, wrapping it tightly in the opposite direction.

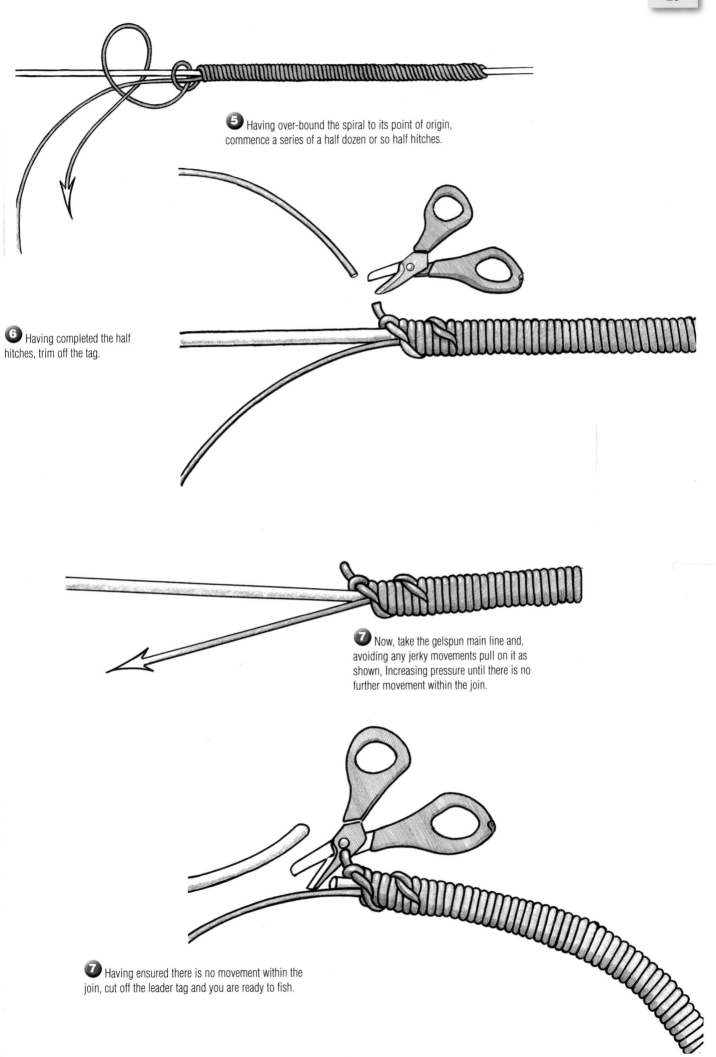

5 Having over-bound the spiral to its point of origin, commence a series of a half dozen or so half hitches.

6 Having completed the half hitches, trim off the tag.

7 Now, take the gelspun main line and, avoiding any jerky movements pull on it as shown, Increasing pressure until there is no further movement within the join.

7 Having ensured there is no movement within the join, cut off the leader tag and you are ready to fish.

NAIL KNOTTING DOUBLE TO LEADER

This is a particularly effective method of attaching a twisted monofilament double, or gelspun double, to a heavier monofilament leader. You will need a rigid tube or similar device to tie this knot.

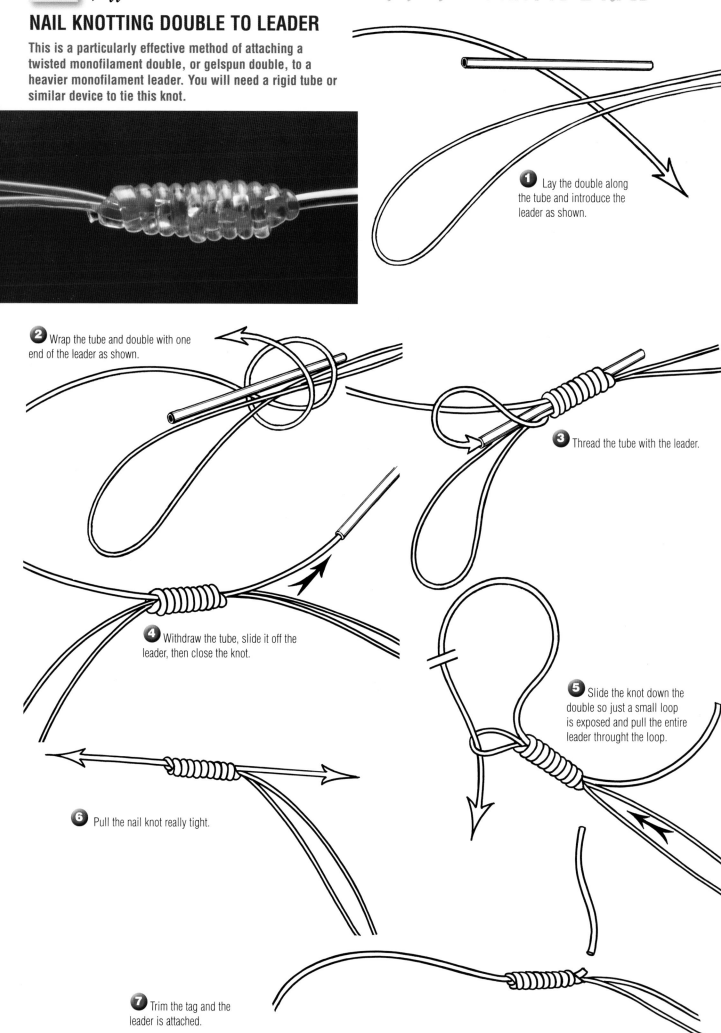

1 Lay the double along the tube and introduce the leader as shown.

2 Wrap the tube and double with one end of the leader as shown.

3 Thread the tube with the leader.

4 Withdraw the tube, slide it off the leader, then close the knot.

5 Slide the knot down the double so just a small loop is exposed and pull the entire leader throught the loop.

6 Pull the nail knot really tight.

7 Trim the tag and the leader is attached.

SHOCK TIPPET AND LEADER KNOT

This is one of the strongest method for connecting a class tippet to a shock tippet, without first securing a double with either a Bimini or plait, that I have tested. It also provides a strong join between a monofilament main line and a heavier leader and is particularly useful for making wind-on leaders.

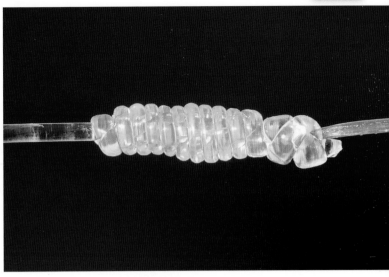

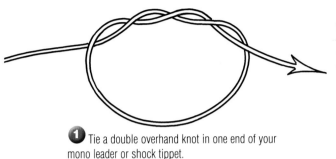

1 Tie a double overhand knot in one end of your mono leader or shock tippet.

2 Tension the knot to the point where a double loop is formed but no more.

3 Thread the class tippet or mono main line through the double loop configuration as shown.

4 Pull the double overhand knot in the heavy line really tight so that some flattening or deformity is noticeable.

5 We need to tie a nail knot in the class tippet or mono main line using a fine metal tube. I use a Lumbar Puncture which is a coarse surgical needle. I have also used a 1/16" OD, K&S brass tube, like those used in model aircraft.

6 Wrap you tube or needle with the class tippet or mono main line eleven or twelve times.

7 Then thread the class tippet or mono main line into the tube.

8 Slide the tube out from under the wraps.

9 Slide the two knots together. Close up the nail knot but don't pull it too tight or you could break the class tippet and have to start again.

10 Trim the tags and the attachment is complete.

I tested this knot using a connection between a class tippet line marked Stren, High Impact, Hard Mono Leader, 20 lb Test, Dia. .022" (0.55 mm), and a heavier line marked Jinkai 150 lb, Dia. 1.04 mm (.04"). In the first test the class tippet broke within the knot at 9.1 kg (20 lbs). In the second test the class tippet broke within the knot at 9.25 kg (20.38 lbs).

LOOP AND CROSS LOOP CONNECTIONS

Loop & Cross Loop Connections are used for joining two lines, each with a loop at the end to be joined. In this case, a Wind-on Leader, which has been loop-spliced at one end, is being attached to a short Bimini double in the end of the line coming from the reel: There are other applications as well.

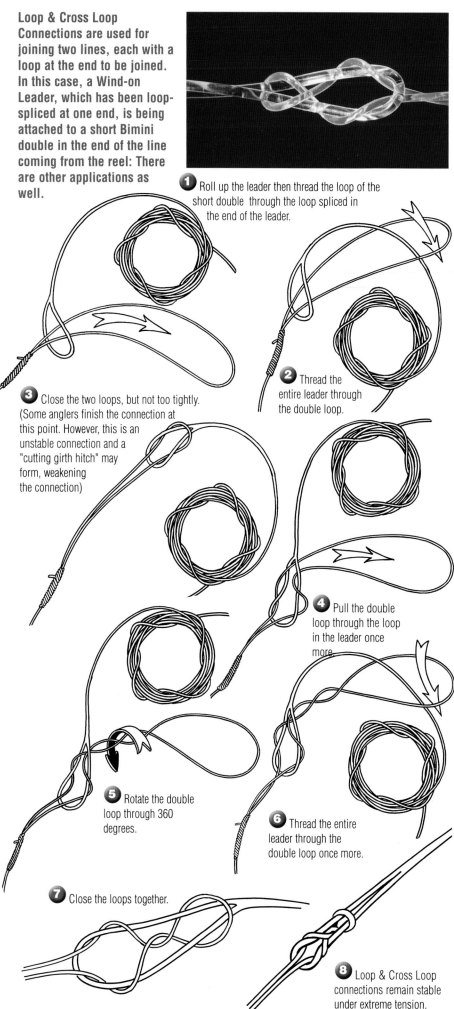

1 Roll up the leader then thread the loop of the short double through the loop spliced in the end of the leader.

2 Thread the entire leader through the double loop.

3 Close the two loops, but not too tightly. (Some anglers finish the connection at this point. However, this is an unstable connection and a "cutting girth hitch" may form, weakening the connection)

4 Pull the double loop through the loop in the leader once more.

5 Rotate the double loop through 360 degrees.

6 Thread the entire leader through the double loop once more.

7 Close the loops together.

8 Loop & Cross Loop connections remain stable under extreme tension.

DARRYL BRANDON'S LEADER KNOT

Demonstrated by Charter boat skipper Darryl Brandon, this secure connection between a monofilament main line and heavier leader is somewhat similar to an Albright Knot except that, in this case, it is the lighter main line that is doubled over into a loop and the leader wrapped around it.

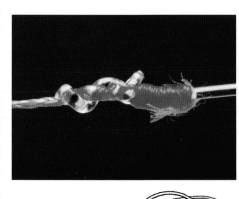

1 Double main line into a loop, thread it with the leader and wrap the loop.

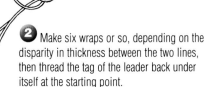

2 Make six wraps or so, depending on the disparity in thickness between the two lines, then thread the tag of the leader back under itself at the starting point.

3 Close the knot by pulling gently on the leader against the main line, first as a loop, before releasing the tag as the knot tightens.

4 The finished knot should look something like this.

DACRON
JOINS & SPLICES

WIND ON DACRON LEADER SPLICE

Described is the process of threading a heavy monofilament leader into the free end of a dacron fishing line so it may be wound through the rod guides and onto the reel. The leader is usually from five to ten metres in length and twice to three times the breaking strain of the dacron.

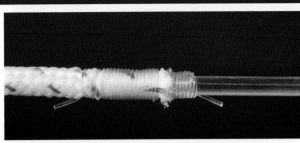

1 Sharpen the end of the monofilament leader to a point, but don't make it sharp enough to spear through the weave of the dacron.

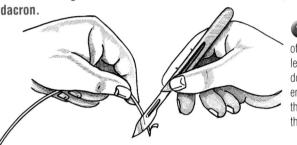

2 Remove any rough edges using fine sandpaper.

3 Push the tapered end of the monofilament leader inside the hollow dacron line.

4 Work the mono up inside the dacron by alternately bunching up the dacron over the mono, then stretching it out again.

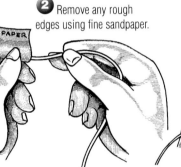

5 Having pushed the mono some 30 cm or so inside the dacron line, trim the frayed dacron ends.

6 Take a length of fine thread, tie a loop in one end, then cut the loop off to use a pull-through to finish off the binding. Then commence a firm binding on the join.

Having threaded the monofilament leader into the dacron as described, it can't be pulled out. This is because pulling on the dacron contracts the weave, holding the monofilament firm. However, the mono may be released by pushing the dacron off so the weave expands. For this reason we must put a binding on the join. Fine waxed thread is most often recommended, but I now use a fine gelspun fishing line like Gorilla Braid or Spectra with a nominated breaking strain of 20 or 30 pounds.

7 Having secured the join, over-bind the loop you made for at least the same distance as the existing binding, then thread the tag through the loop.

9 Pull the binding tight, trim the tags, then saturate the entire binding with a pliable rubber sealant like Pliobond or Aquaseal.

8 Extract the loop, and the tag.

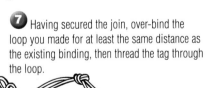

CAUTION: The join between leader and line is now secure. However, separation may occur when rigging skirted trolling heads directly onto the leader. This is because a hooked fish taking line causes the lure to run back to the splice. While this is itself would not cause a separation, a situation which can occur—and one which I have experienced personally—is the lure riding backwards, hard up against the joining splice, may be struck by another game fish, and with sufficient force, to cause a separation.

WIND ON LEADERS FOR GAME FISHING

This version of Steve Morris' Top Shot, Wind-on Leader features "Shigeshi Tanaka's Loop Splice," an innovation which holds the dacron loop firmly in place, a most desirable feature when large fish need to be played out over a long period of time. Although you can use a doubled length of single strand wire as a needle, this connection is best performed using the Top Shot dacron splicing needles produced by Top Shot Tackle in South Australia who export most of their products to the United States. Top Shot glues are recommended for sealing the splice, but suitable alternatives include Aquaseal and Pliobond.

Other materials include a five to ten metre length of monofilament three to five times the breaking strain of the line already on the reel, and some hollow dacron line about twice the breaking strain of the line on the reel. There is room for some variation with sleeve and leader size, but heavier, or lighter monofilament leaders, require a compatible dacron sleeve.

You will also need a sharp knife or scalpel for sharpening one end of the monofilament leader, and loop gauge or pencil to keep your loop open. A fine waxed thread, or other strong binding thread, is used for finishing off.

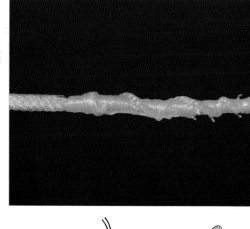

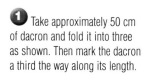

1 Take approximately 50 cm of dacron and fold it into three as shown. Then mark the dacron a third the way along its length.

2 Put the dacron sleeve aside for the present, and sharpen the heavy monofilament leader to a point with your knife or scalpel.

3 Having sharpened your leader to a fairly fine point, insert it into the hollow end of your end-splicing needle.
The end-splicing needle is to allow you to thread the heavy monofilament up the hollow dacron. However, with a little practise, you will probably be able to thread the dacron sleeve with the heavy mono without using the needle.

4 Take up the dacron once more and thread your loop-splicing needle through the weave of the dacron at your one third mark. Then thread the eye of the needle with the short end of the dacron.

5 Pull the short end through the dacron so a loop is formed.

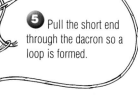

6 Thread the loop splicing needle through the short end this time, right up next to the loop, and thread the eye of the needle with the long end of the dacron. Then pull the long end through the short end.

7 Repeat this procedure until four stitches have been made, alternating stitches with the long and short ends of the dacron.

8 Thread your loop-spicing needle inside the long end of the dacron; then thread the eye of the needle with the short end of the dacron.

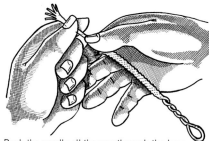

9 Push the needle all the way through the long end of the dacron so that the short end tag emerges from the long end which is now bunched up to less than half its original length over the short end.

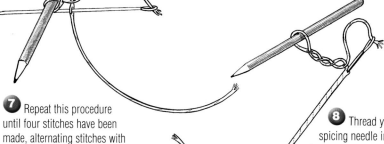

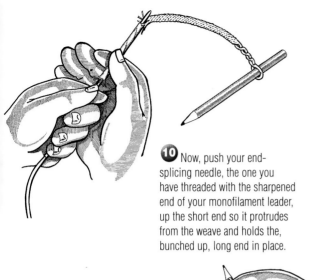

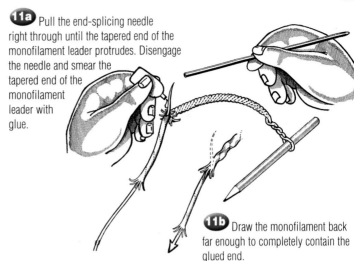

11a Pull the end-splicing needle right through until the tapered end of the monofilament leader protrudes. Disengage the needle and smear the tapered end of the monofilament leader with glue.

10 Now, push your end-splicing needle, the one you have threaded with the sharpened end of your monofilament leader, up the short end so it protrudes from the weave and holds the, bunched up, long end in place.

11b Draw the monofilament back far enough to completely contain the glued end.

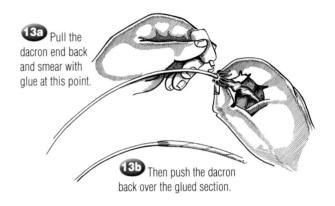

12 Now push the external two thirds of the dacron right down over the internal join between dacron and monofilament.

13a Pull the dacron end back and smear with glue at this point.

13b Then push the dacron back over the glued section.

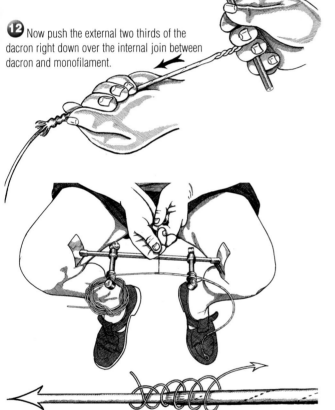

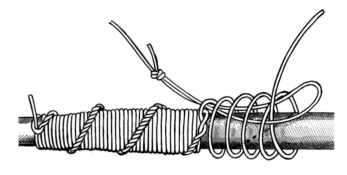

14 Stretch the leader out really tight using either a Top Shot Spreader Jig (illustrated), or other suitable means. Then, with your waxed thread, make a clove hitch on the monofilament just below the dacron, and continue making a series of firm half hitches back up the monofilament and over the dacron end.

15 Continue thus until the waxed thread binding extends a similar distance each side of the dacron end, over-bind a loop of thread so you can use it a pull-through to finish off your binding.

16 Extract your pull-through, and with it the tag. Close the binding with firm pressure on the tag.

17 The finished splice should look like this and pass easily through the line guides and onto your reel. Connection is achieved by first tying a very short double or end loop in you main line, then interlocking the loop in the leader with a Cat's Paw or Loop and Cross Loop connection.
Use at least one coat of waterproof sealant like Top Shot Dac Tac, Aquaseal or Pliobond and allow to cure.

CAUTION:
The join between leader and line is now secure: However, separation may occur when rigging skirted trolling heads directly onto the leader. This is because a hooked fish taking line causes the lure to run back to the splice. While this is itself would not cause a separation, a situation which can occur - and one which I have experienced personally - is the lure riding backwards, hard up against the joining splice, may be struck by another game fish, and with sufficient force, to cause a separation.

WIND ON WIRE LEADERS

This method of rigging full-length IGFA wind-on wire leaders was devised by Steve Morris of Top Shot Tackle in Adelaide Australia. Nylon or plastic coated, 49 strand cable is best.

The specimen used for these illustrations was rigged from 400 pound, nylon coated, 49 strand cable and 130 pound IGFA dacron. A Top Shot, loop splicing needle was used to make the loop in the dacron sleeve, but you can use a doubled length of single strand wire as a substitute.

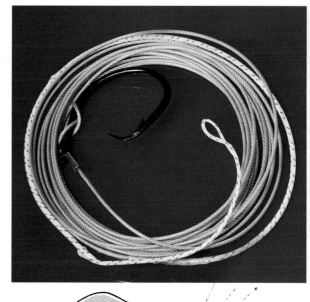

Preparation of the Wire

1 Remove the last couple of centimetres of nylon or plastic coating from the wire.

2 Saturate the exposed strand with Super Glue.

3 Allow the strands to fuse, then shave the fused strands to a taper using a belt sander like I did or similar device.

These first three steps prepare the wire so it will slide into the dacron sleeve without catching. However, because there may be some loose strands, it is advisable to give the wire another application of Super Glue and a sprinkling of talcum powder to make it smooth. An alternate treatment is to use Hot Melt Glue to cover the exposed wire taper and allow it to cool.

Preparation of the Sleeve

4 Take about 50 cm (20 inches) of 130 pound IGFA dacron and fold it into three roughly equal lengths, then mark one of the folds.

5 Take an object to use as a loop gauge like a pencil or a pen, pass one third of the line around it and push your loop splicing needle or doubled wire through at the mark you made in the previous step.

6 Pull the dacron end through.

7 Now, thread the dacron splicing needle sideways through the weave of the short end, the opposite end to the one you threaded before.

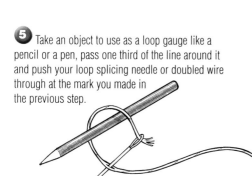

8 Pull the long end through, then thread the needle sideways through the weave of the long end once more.

9 Finally, the loop splicing needle, or doubled wire, is threaded length wise through the long end of the dacron so the short end can be drawn right through.

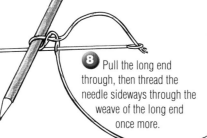

10 Draw out the short end so the long end is now bunched up over the short end.

11 The bunched long end is secured in place, by a large paper clip in this case, and the tapered end of the wire is pushed into the short end of the dacron sleeve.

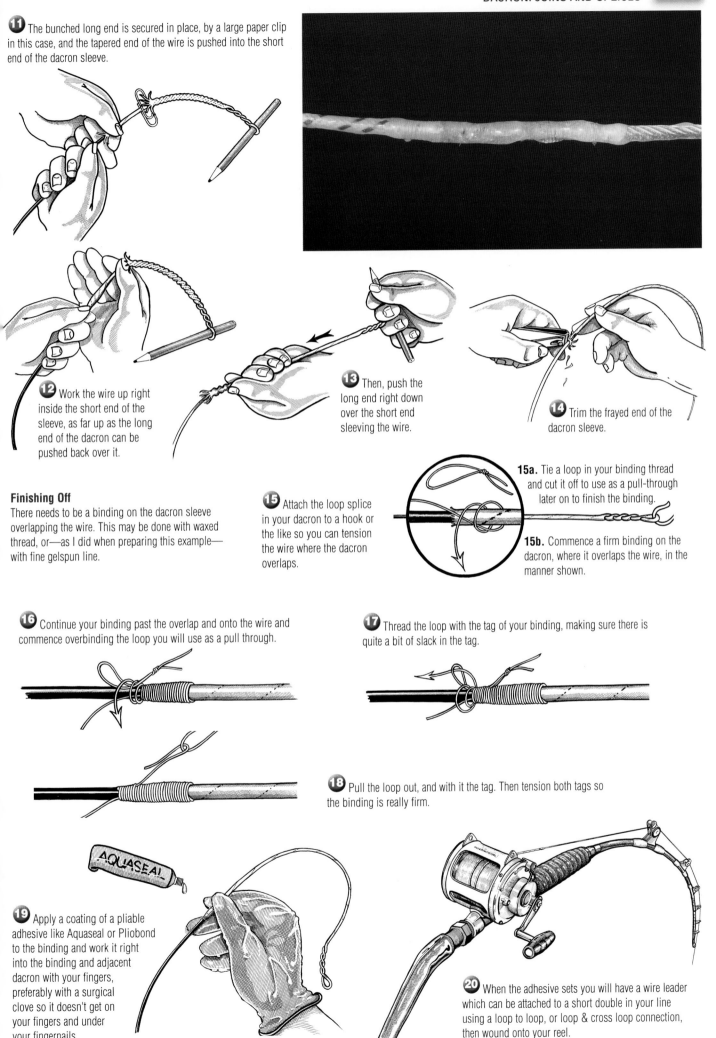

12 Work the wire up right inside the short end of the sleeve, as far up as the long end of the dacron can be pushed back over it.

13 Then, push the long end right down over the short end sleeving the wire.

14 Trim the frayed end of the dacron sleeve.

Finishing Off

There needs to be a binding on the dacron sleeve overlapping the wire. This may be done with waxed thread, or—as I did when preparing this example—with fine gelspun line.

15 Attach the loop splice in your dacron to a hook or the like so you can tension the wire where the dacron overlaps.

15a. Tie a loop in your binding thread and cut it off to use as a pull-through later on to finish the binding.

15b. Commence a firm binding on the dacron, where it overlaps the wire, in the manner shown.

16 Continue your binding past the overlap and onto the wire and commence overbinding the loop you will use as a pull through.

17 Thread the loop with the tag of your binding, making sure there is quite a bit of slack in the tag.

18 Pull the loop out, and with it the tag. Then tension both tags so the binding is really firm.

19 Apply a coating of a pliable adhesive like Aquaseal or Pliobond to the binding and work it right into the binding and adjacent dacron with your fingers, preferably with a surgical clove so it doesn't get on your fingers and under your fingernails.

20 When the adhesive sets you will have a wire leader which can be attached to a short double in your line using a loop to loop, or loop & cross loop connection, then wound onto your reel.

DACRON JOINING SPLICE

This method of joining two lengths of IGFA, line class dacron, is used and recommended by Steve Morris of Top Shot Tackle in South Australia. A dacron splicing needle is required.

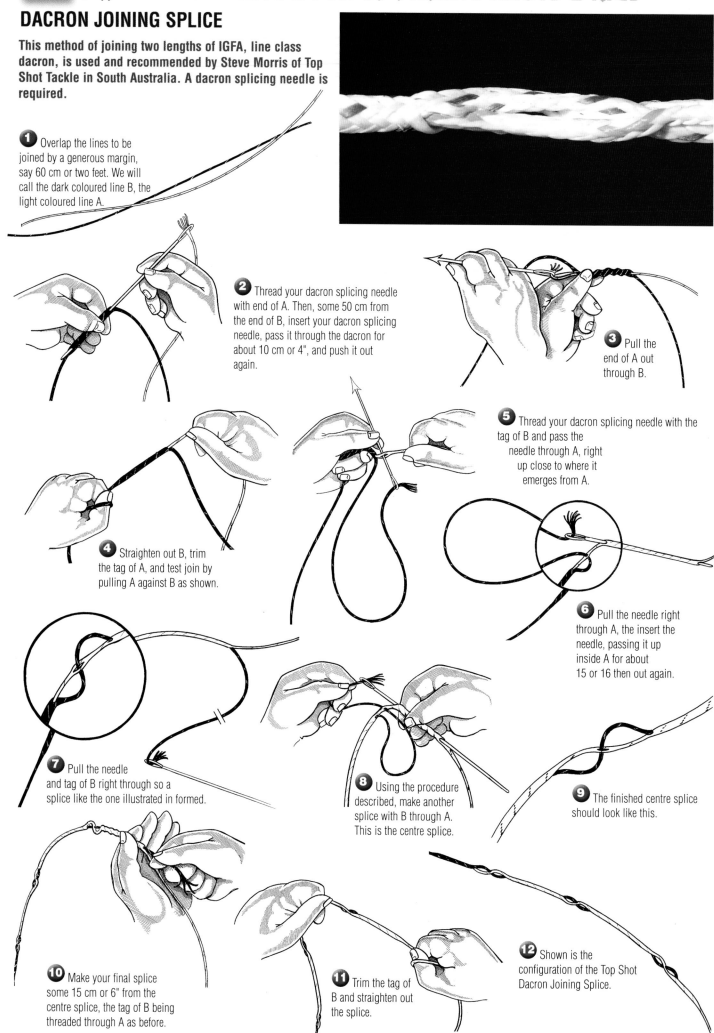

1 Overlap the lines to be joined by a generous margin, say 60 cm or two feet. We will call the dark coloured line B, the light coloured line A.

2 Thread your dacron splicing needle with end of A. Then, some 50 cm from the end of B, insert your dacron splicing needle, pass it through the dacron for about 10 cm or 4", and push it out again.

3 Pull the end of A out through B.

4 Straighten out B, trim the tag of A, and test join by pulling A against B as shown.

5 Thread your dacron splicing needle with the tag of B and pass the needle through A, right up close to where it emerges from A.

6 Pull the needle right through A, the insert the needle, passing it up inside A for about 15 or 16 then out again.

7 Pull the needle and tag of B right through so a splice like the one illustrated in formed.

8 Using the procedure described, make another splice with B through A. This is the centre splice.

9 The finished centre splice should look like this.

10 Make your final splice some 15 cm or 6" from the centre splice, the tag of B being threaded through A as before.

11 Trim the tag of B and straighten out the splice.

12 Shown is the configuration of the Top Shot Dacron Joining Splice.

TANAKA'S LOOP

This method of splicing a loop in dacron, heavy gelspun or other hollow braided leader material, was created by celebrated stand-up game fisherman, Shigeshi Tanaka, of Japan. This loop is totally secure with no movement at all making it ideal for the Cat's Paw, and similar connections used with wind-on leaders. It is best performed using a Top Shot dacron loop-splicing needle made by Top Shot Tackle, Australia.

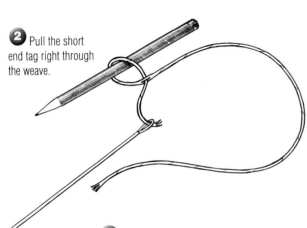

1 Select a length of dacron or other hollow braided line of suitable diameter for the wind-on leader you intend building. Pass the loop-splicing needle through the weave, more or less at right angles, about one third the way along, and thread the needle with the short end tag. The pencil represents the need to hold the loop open during the initial stages of forming the splice.

2 Pull the short end tag right through the weave.

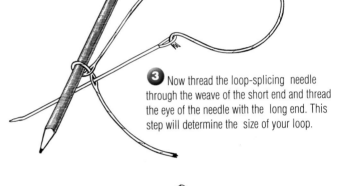

3 Now thread the loop-splicing needle through the weave of the short end and thread the eye of the needle with the long end. This step will determine the size of your loop.

4 Continue in the same manner, alternately threading each end through the weave of the opposite length making each stitch as close to the last as you can manage.

5 The splice may be finished off by simply trimming the short tag after the third stitch, or . . .

6 You can thread the loop splicing needle with the tag or the short end and pull it down inside the long end.

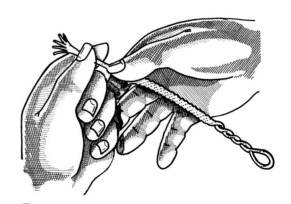

7 Having pushed your needle down through the longer length of the dacron, which is now bunched over the shorter length, you may follow from step 9 on page 26 to complete the Top Shot wind-on leader.

DOUBLES

PLAITING A DOUBLE

Although plaiting is considered a little too slow and inconvenient for most sportfishing situations it is the most satisfactory way of tying a full length I.G.F.A. double, retaining the full breaking strain of the line being used. This is how it is done.

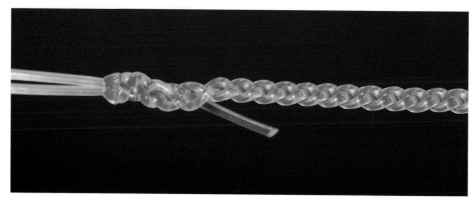

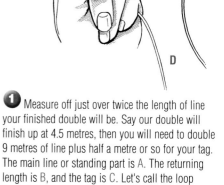

1 Measure off just over twice the length of line your finished double will be. Say our double will finish up at 4.5 metres, then you will need to double 9 metres of line plus half a metre or so for your tag. The main line or standing part is A. The returning length is B, and the tag is C. Let's call the loop formed, D.

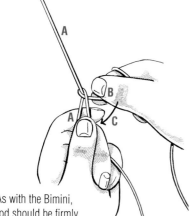

2 As with the Bimini, your rod should be firmly in a rod holder and the clutch of the reel set on strike drag. Keeping the line tight by pulling away from your rod and reel, pass C over B (alongside A). Pull B tight. Because tension must be maintained throughout the plaiting process, it helps to wrap each successive leg in turn, around your finger as shown.

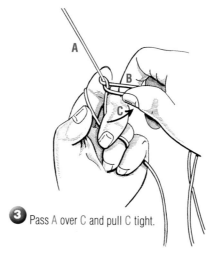

3 Pass A over C and pull C tight.

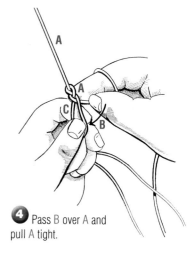

4 Pass B over A and pull A tight.

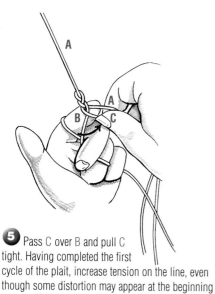

5 Pass C over B and pull C tight. Having completed the first cycle of the plait, increase tension on the line, even though some distortion may appear at the beginning of the plait. This is normal.

6 Now you are getting the idea, A goes over C then C is pulled tight. Always pull the leg you have just crossed, really tight against the line coming from your rod and reel. That way your plait will be nice and firm.

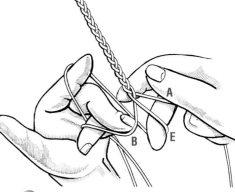

7 Having plaited for at least a dozen cycles, or what appears to be far enough say 5 cm for 10 kg, 8 cm for 15 kg, 12 cm for 24 kg and so on double the tag over to form loop E as shown.

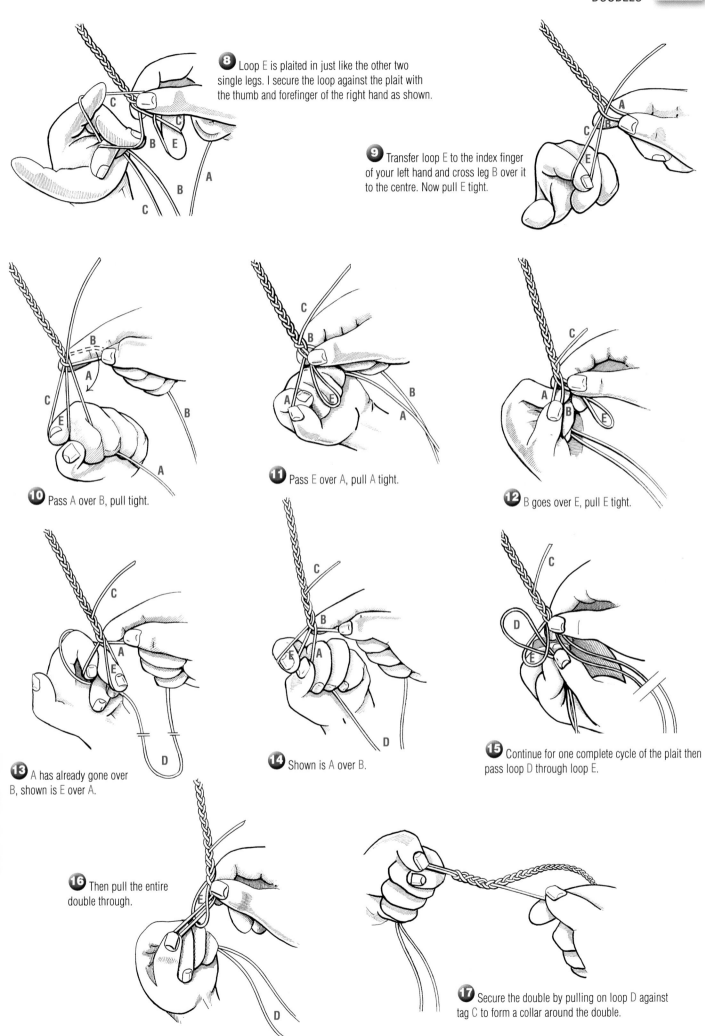

8 Loop E is plaited in just like the other two single legs. I secure the loop against the plait with the thumb and forefinger of the right hand as shown.

9 Transfer loop E to the index finger of your left hand and cross leg B over it to the centre. Now pull E tight.

10 Pass A over B, pull tight.

11 Pass E over A, pull A tight.

12 B goes over E, pull E tight.

13 A has already gone over B, shown is E over A.

14 Shown is A over B.

15 Continue for one complete cycle of the plait then pass loop D through loop E.

16 Then pull the entire double through.

17 Secure the double by pulling on loop D against tag C to form a collar around the double.

BIMINI TWIST

Short doubles or end loops like those used in sport and fly fishing, are easily secured with a Bimini Twist which retains the full breaking strain of monofilament and most other lines.

Several ways of tying a Bimini Twist have evolved. The method shown here, with the rod placed firmly in a rod holder, is easiest to master and should enable the angler to graduate, more easily, to hand-tensioned Biminis later on.

1a Thread the line through your line guides of your rod and place your rod securely in a rod holder with your reel on strike drag.

1b Tie a small loop in the end of your line, then cut it off and put it aside. This is to act as a pull-through to finish off the Bimini later on.

2 Make a loop in the end of your line and roll in at least 20 twists (I prefer at least 30). In this drawing, the twists are made in a clockwise direction.

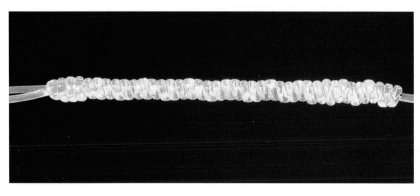

3 Place the loop you have just formed over your foot.

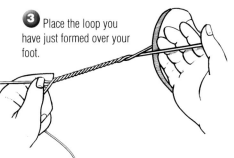

4a Keeping the maximum tension on your line that your drag setting allows, compress the twists tightly together.

4b Fold the tag back so it will spiral back over the twists as you increase tension with your right hand.

5a Shown is the tag spiralling back over the twists.

5b Shown is this effect in close-up.

6 Allow the tag to spiral right up to the crotch in the double and insert the short loop of line marked 1B as a pull-through.

7a Over-bind the pull-through three or four times, taking care to continue (in this case) anti-clockwise, then thread the tag through the loop in the pull-through.

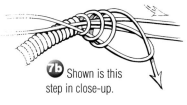

7b Shown is this step in close-up.

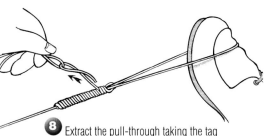

8 Extract the pull-through taking the tag back through the last few wraps.

9a Pull gently, but firmly, on the tag and rotate the Bimini (anti-clockwise) until several twists form in the loop. Don't pull too hard on the tag because you may shear it off and have to retie the whole thing again.

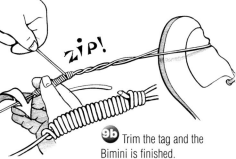

ZIP!

9b Trim the tag and the Bimini is finished.

HAND TENSIONED BIMINI DOUBLE

We have already discovered how to tie a Bimini double with the rod in a rod-holder to tension the line. Now we examine how to tie a hand-tensioned Bimini.

1a Begin by tying a small loop in the end of your line then cutting it off. You will need this loop as a pull-through to finish off the Bimini later on, so don't lose it.

1b Take a loop of line and secure the standing part by taking a bight of line around your left hand.

2 Roll in at least thirty twists.

3 Pass the loop over your shoe, or any convenient fixture like a rod holder in a boat, and keep tension on the loop so it won't come off.

4 Keeping pressure on the standing part, rotate the tag between thumb and forefinger of the right hand to make the tag spiral back over the twists.

5 Hold the tag between thumb and middle finger of the left hand and put your right hand inside the loop over your shoe and open the loop by spreading your fingers and sliding your right hand toward the left hand.
This will cause the tag to spiral back over the twists while tension on the tag is controlled by the pressure of your thumb against the middle finger.

6 When the tag has spiralled back to the crotch in the loop, place your left index finger in the crotch to secure the tag. Then take the small loop you first made and commence wrapping it with the tag.

7 Wrap the loop, and both strands of the Bimini, three or four times then pass the tag through the loop.

8 Withdraw your loop, drawing the tag back out from under the last few wraps.

9 Pull gently on the tag, rotating the Bimini as you do so until a couple of twists appear in the loop, then stop. If you pull tag out too far you will shorten the splice.

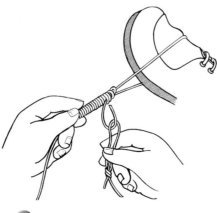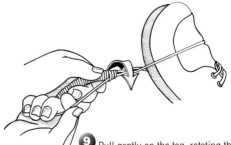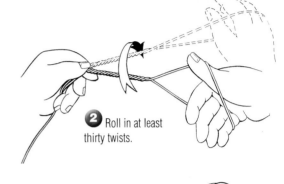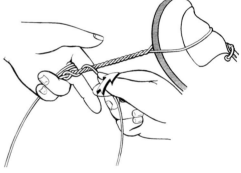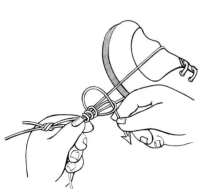

TWISTED DOUBLE

Fusing both strands of monofilament double protects the integrity of each strand and increases the double's elasticity or ability to stretch.

Shown is a method of accomplishing a Twisted Double by twisting the line to produce the spontaneous fusion of both strands. You will need an assistant to perform this operation.

You will also need a secure rod holder, a hand drill with a hook (one can be fashioned from heavy gauge wire), a loop gauge (a pen or pencil will do), and a marking pen—which can double as your loop gauge—or you can use a rubber band. Should you be working with very heavy line you may also need a slim metal tube large enough to accommodate the diameter of the line.

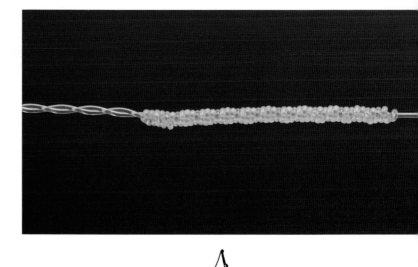

1 This diagram represents the following:

- Rod placed in a secure rod holder
- A length of line pulled from the reel representing two and a half times the required length of the double.
- An overhand loop tied in the end of that line so it can be twisted with the hand drill and hook combination.

2 Engaging strike drag on the reel, and keeping the line reasonably tight between the hook in the drill chuck and the rod, your assistant will need to wind the handle of the drill to twist the line.

The number of twists will depend on the length of the line between rod tip and drill. For 15 metres (about 50 feet), 1500 twists would not be excessive and—depending on the gear ratio of the drill—would probably require between 300 and 500 rotations of the handle. Check the gear ratio of the drill and do the arithmetic.

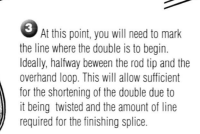

3 At this point, you will need to mark the line where the double is to begin. Ideally, halfway beween the rod tip and the overhand loop. This will allow sufficient for the shortening of the double due to it being twisted and the amount of line required for the finishing splice.

3a Here also is where you must decide whether to simply produce a Twisted Double, which does not presentthe ideal medium for tying off to aswivel or the like, or whether to tiein at this point a straight endloop, preferably using the Nail Knot and Loop I have illustrated, to facilitate a better medium for such attachments.

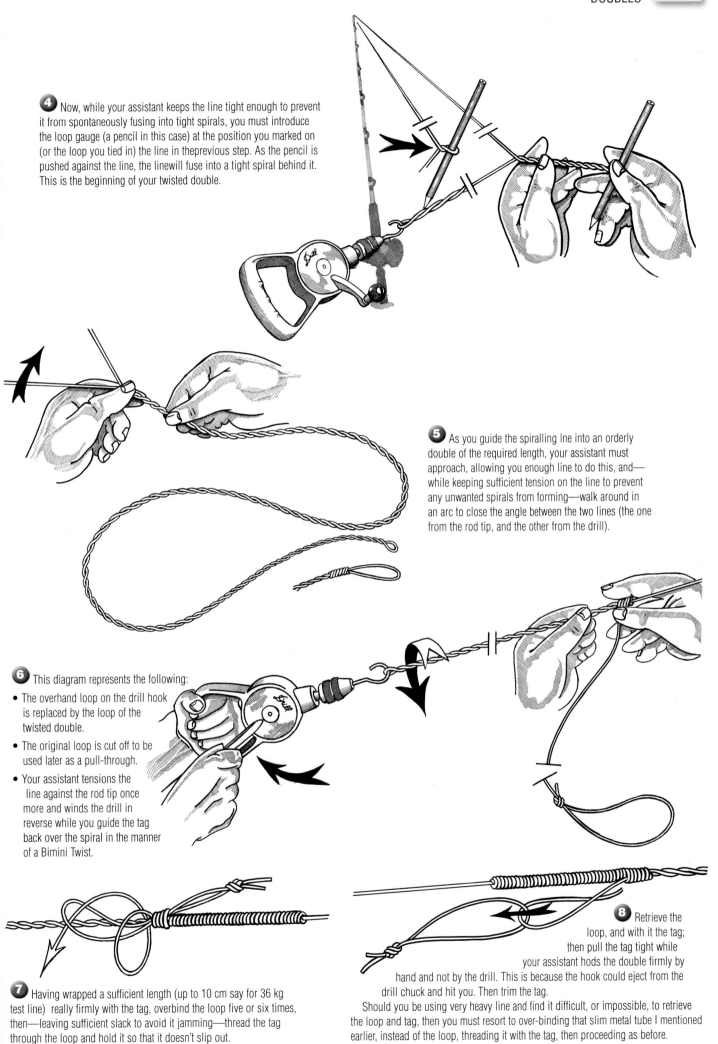

4 Now, while your assistant keeps the line tight enough to prevent it from spontaneously fusing into tight spirals, you must introduce the loop gauge (a pencil in this case) at the position you marked on (or the loop you tied in) the line in the previous step. As the pencil is pushed against the line, the line will fuse into a tight spiral behind it. This is the beginning of your twisted double.

5 As you guide the spiralling line into an orderly double of the required length, your assistant must approach, allowing you enough line to do this, and—while keeping sufficient tension on the line to prevent any unwanted spirals from forming—walk around in an arc to close the angle between the two lines (the one from the rod tip, and the other from the drill).

6 This diagram represents the following:
- The overhand loop on the drill hook is replaced by the loop of the twisted double.
- The original loop is cut off to be used later as a pull-through.
- Your assistant tensions the line against the rod tip once more and winds the drill in reverse while you guide the tag back over the spiral in the manner of a Bimini Twist.

7 Having wrapped a sufficient length (up to 10 cm say for 36 kg test line) really firmly with the tag, overbind the loop five or six times, then—leaving sufficient slack to avoid it jamming—thread the tag through the loop and hold it so that it doesn't slip out.

8 Retrieve the loop, and with it the tag; then pull the tag tight while your assistant holds the double firmly by hand and not by the drill. This is because the hook could eject from the drill chuck and hit you. Then trim the tag.

Should you be using very heavy line and find it difficult, or impossible, to retrieve the loop and tag, then you must resort to over-binding that slim metal tube I mentioned earlier, instead of the loop, threading it with the tag, then proceeding as before.

SPIDER HITCH

Unlike the Bimini Twist and Plait, which are progressive splices, the Spider Hitch is a knot, which retains around 80% of line strength in monofilament. However, tied in gelspun lines it retains only 40 to 60% of the actual breaking strain.

Although lacking the strength of the Bimini and Plait the Spider Hitch does produce a double strand with which to attach terminals and leaders and it is quick and easy to tie.

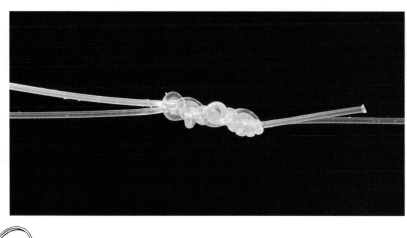

1 Having determined the size of your double or end loop, twist in a second loop just above the tag end and hold it between the thumb and finger of your left hand.

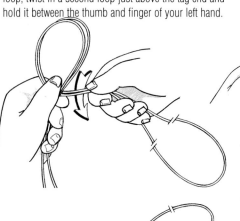

2 Wind the double around the thumb of your left hand.

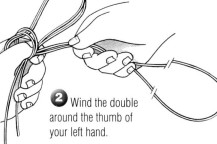

3 Make four or five complete wraps.

4 Then pass the loop in the double through the second loop.

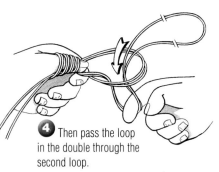

5 Pinching thumb and finger of the left hand firmly together so the loops disengage one at a time, pull gently but firmly on the double until all the loops have slid from your left thumb.

6 Tension all four strands equally and your Spider Hitch should look something like this.

NAIL KNOT & LOOP

Sometimes eferred to as Nail Knot with a Loop, this is the most satisactory way of producing an end loop in a Twisted Double and is the knot referred to in step 3b of same.

1 At the point required, form this double loop configuration, with one loop larger than the other.

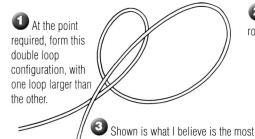

2 Wrap the smaller loop by rotating the larger loop around it.

3 Shown is what I believe is the most satisactory way of accomplishing this.

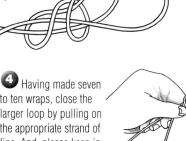

4 Having made seven to ten wraps, close the larger loop by pulling on the appropriate strand of line. And, please keep in mind which strand this is. We'd better call it strand B and the other, strand A.

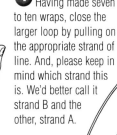

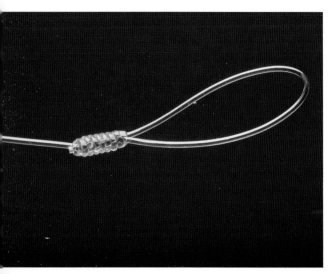

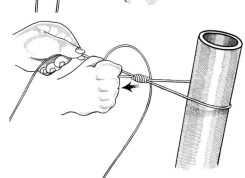

5 Tease out the small loop to the required size and place it over a pipe or other fixture; a gaff pole in a rod holder would probably do. Then, while keeping some tension on strand A, increase tension on strand B until the knot locks in place with a definite click.

Now you may proceed with step 4 in tying the Twisted Double.

KNOTS

DUNCAN'S LOOP

Sometimes confused with the Uni Knot which looks similar but is not the same, Duncan's Loop provides a simple fixed loop attachment for fly to tippet or hook to leader. Peter Hayes of "Guided Fishing" provided the demonstration on which these drawings are based.

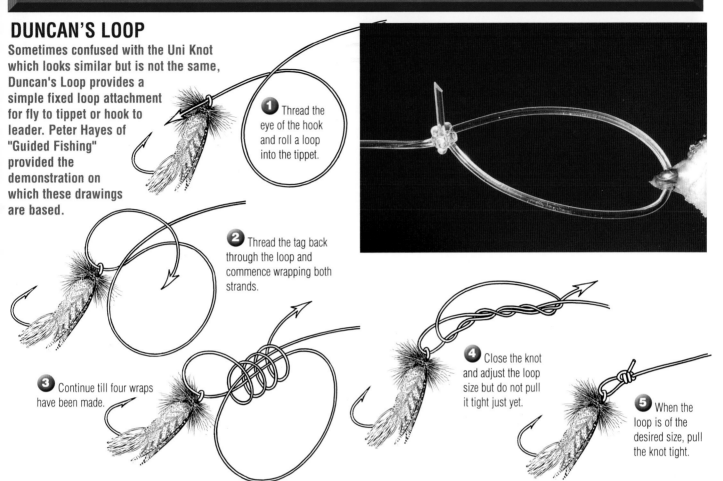

1 Thread the eye of the hook and roll a loop into the tippet.

2 Thread the tag back through the loop and commence wrapping both strands.

3 Continue till four wraps have been made.

4 Close the knot and adjust the loop size but do not pull it tight just yet.

5 When the loop is of the desired size, pull the knot tight.

LEFTY'S LOOP

When desirable for the fly to have free movement at the end of the tippet, it is rigged on a small loop. This knot is easy to tie and retains a substantial percentage of the line's breaking strain.

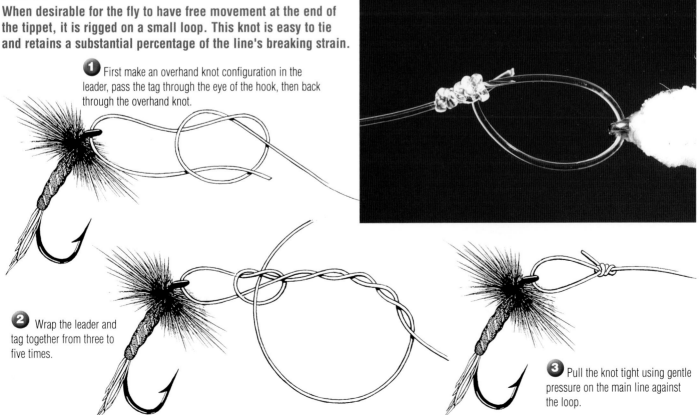

1 First make an overhand knot configuration in the leader, pass the tag through the eye of the hook, then back through the overhand knot.

2 Wrap the leader and tag together from three to five times.

3 Pull the knot tight using gentle pressure on the main line against the loop.

IMPROVED TURLE KNOT

This knot provides a strong, neat connection to flies tied on hooks with turned-down eyes.

1 Thread the tippet trough the eye of the hook and over the body of the fly.

2 Then thread the tippet back through the eye of the hook.

3 Tie and overhand knot in the tag around the standing part of the tippet.

4 Add a second wrap to the overhand knot.

5 Close the overhand knot, but do not pull it really tight yet.

6 Pull the knot up with gentle pressure on the tippet so the knot slides right down into the eye of the hook.

Pull the knot up tight and trim the tag.

BLOOD KNOT

Possibly the strongest method of attaching a fly to a monofilament leader is the Blood knot. It differs from the Half Blood in that the line is passed through the eye of the hook twice. This limits its use on very small hook eyes.

To retain the full potential strength of this knot, the loop sequence on the eye of the hook must be retained until the knot is pulled tight.

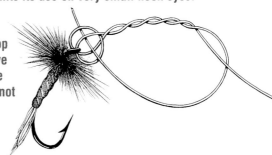

HALF BLOOD KNOT

The simplest, and most commonly used knot for attaching flies is the simple Half Blood. This knot should be used with caution, because under some circumstances it is inclined to slip.

This knot is tied by passing the line through the eye of the hook, wrapping the tag around the main line three to six times, then passing the tag back through the first loop made around the eye of the hook. The finer the diameter of the line in relation to the diameter of the hook eye, the greater the number of turns (up to six), that should be made.

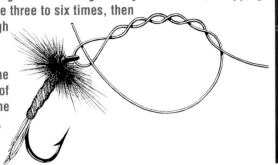

LOCKED HALF BLOOD KNOT

The Half Blood can be locked so that it won't slip. This is done by first forming the knot, then tucking the tag back through the transverse loop before pulling the knot up tight.

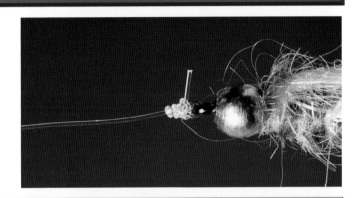

ATTACHING FLY LINE TO HOLLOW BRAID BACKING

This method of attaching a fly line to a hollow braided backing is used and recommended by Rob Meade of Clear Water Tours.

1 The fly line has to go inside the hollow backing so it is advisable to first insert a coarse needle inside the backing to open the weave.

3 You won't be able to pull the fly line out from the backing because the increased tension makes the backing contract. However, the fly line can easily removed by pushing the backing off the fly line. To prevent this from happening we make a lashing with very fine fishing line, preferably gelspun fishing line, to make the join secure. In this case we over-bind a loop of line to use as a pull-though to finish off.

2 Push the fly line at least two inches (5 cm) inside the backing. You may have to jiggle it back and forth if it gets stuck, but it should go in.

4 Make ten or a dozen wraps over the pull-though loop, then thread the tag through the loop.

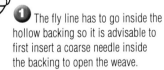

5 Pull the loop out, and with it the tag.

6 Tighten the binding with pressure on both side, trim the tags and backing fringe with a set of nail clippers, the cover the lashing with a waterproof sealant like Aquaseal or Pliobond.

MONOFILAMENT LOOP TO FLY LINE

The following process was shown to me by Rob Meade of Clear Water Tours. It enables loop to loop connections with fly leaders in trout fishing.

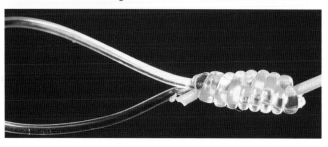

1 Take half a metre or so of monofilament with a diameter of about 0.5 mm and make the double loop configuration shown at the end of your fly line (black). Note that one loop is larger than the other.

2 Wrap the fly line and smaller monofilament loop with the larger monofilament loop.

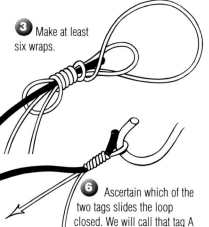

3 Make at least six wraps.

4 Holding the loops together on the fly line so they don't spring apart, hook the smaller loop over a fixed hook or similar object and close the knot by pulling on both tags against the loop, but not too firmly at this stage. This will cause the loops at each end of the knot to close and the loop on the hook to open.

5 At this point you will be aware that one side of the loop is fixed, because it is tied to the fly line, and the other side of the loop will slide because the knot it is simply pinned against the fly line by the knot. Spread a small amount of suitable glue, like "Zap a Gap" on the side of the loop that slides.

6 Ascertain which of the two tags slides the loop closed. We will call that tag A and the other tag, the one forming the knot, tag B. Close the loop on the fixed hook by holding tag A firmly and sliding the loop up on the hook so the glued section is within the knot.

7 Adjust the loop to the size required by alternating tension between tag A and tag B. Then, and this is important, increase pressure on tag B until the knot closes down really firmly on the fly line, pinning the glued side of the loop firmly so it wont slip. Remember, only one side the loop is tied. The loop is secured by the tension of the knot and the glue which you have applied.

8 Trim the tags and protruding fly line and your monofilament loop is complete.

NAIL KNOT USING TUBE

This is an easier way to tie the nail knot for some. It requires a slender, stiff, tube onto which the leader is tied. The fly line is then inserted into the tube and the knot held by the thumb and forefinger while the tube is pulled away, this leaves the knot positioned perfectly over the fly line.

1 Shown is the tube with a monofilament leader coiled beside.

2 Begin wrapping by passing the loop over the tube and tag.

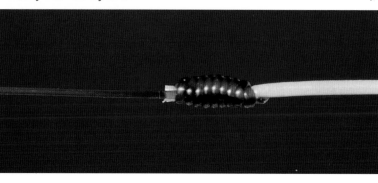

3 Continue to wrap in this way until a snell is formed on the tube.

4 Close the snell tightly on the tube by pulling the tag against the standing part. Then insert the fly line in the tube.

5 Transfer the snell from the tube onto the fly line.

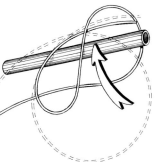

6 Pull the snell up tightly on the fly line so that it bites down into the fly line making a smooth join.

INDICATOR KNOT

This knot produces a sliding loop in the leader for the purpose of securing a small piece of yarn to act as a visible strike indicator.

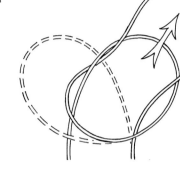

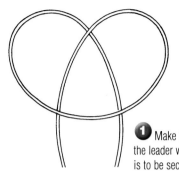

1 Make this configuration in the leader where the indicator is to be secured.

2 Pull one of the crossed legs out through the loop so that another loop is formed with a knot around it.

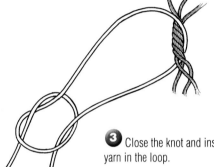

3 Close the knot and insert the piece of yarn in the loop.

4 Close the loop to secure the piece of yarn to the leader.

SURGEONS KNOT FOR ATTACHING DROPPER

The Surgeons Knot is used for building fly fishing leaders and multihook bait catching rigs. It can also be used for attaching a short dropper near the end of your main line. Its chief advantage over other knots used for the same purpose are its simplicity and speed.

    Bear in mind that large loops are easier to work with when tying this knot so dropper or tippet sections should be cut somewhat longer than when using other joins.

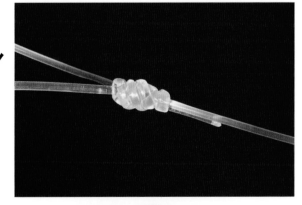

1 Shown is the main line, white, and the tippet or dropper, black. Lay them alongside each other as shown with an overlap of at least 15cm.

2 Tie an overhand knot in both main line and dropper.

3 Make a second wrap in your overhand knot so that four wraps and five crossovers are formed.

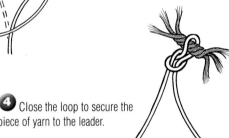

4 With equal pressure on each strand, pull the knot tight. Should the knot fail to close properly, pull gently on each end in turn until the knot is closed before trimming the tag end of the dropper.

HOW TO SPLIT LEADERS

'Splitting' leaders is the term used to describe the process by which one single strand of monofilament becomes two with minimal interruption to the 'lay' of the line, and without significant loss of strength.

This method was shown to me by fellow angling scribe Peter Horrobin who 'splits' flyfishing leaders to present multiple offerings. However, any monofilament line may be 'split' in this manner, either for multiple lure presentation or for rigging with hook and sinker for whiting etc.

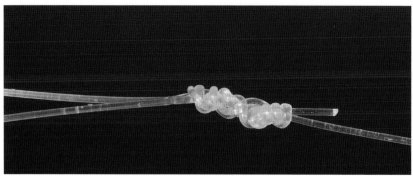

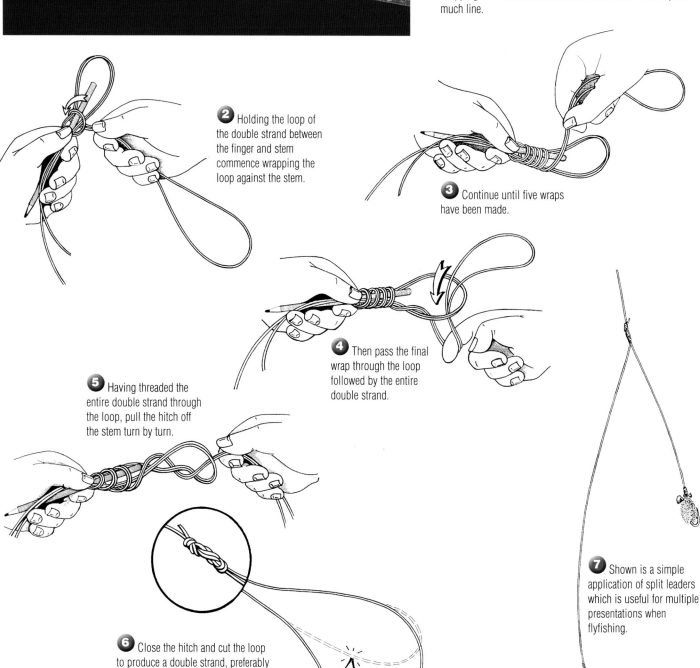

1 Anglers will recognise the configuration of the Spider Hitch, but instead of tying the hitch over our thumb, we use the stem of a float or a pencil (illustrated). The reason why we use a stem and not our thumb is because we are working with considerably shorter lengths of line when splitting leaders than we would be when tying a double for sportfishing, and wrapping the double strand around one's thumb uses up too much line.

2 Holding the loop of the double strand between the finger and stem commence wrapping the loop against the stem.

3 Continue until five wraps have been made.

4 Then pass the final wrap through the loop followed by the entire double strand.

5 Having threaded the entire double strand through the loop, pull the hitch off the stem turn by turn.

6 Close the hitch and cut the loop to produce a double strand, preferably so that one strand is approximately twice as long as the other.

7 Shown is a simple application of split leaders which is useful for multiple presentations when flyfishing.

MAKING SALTWATER FLY FISHING LEADERS

I.G.F.A. makes provision for some saltwater species to be claimed as line class records provided the line class leader and shock tippet (hook length) comply with the following specifications:

The line class leader be at least 15 inches in length measured between any knot, splice or loop.

The shock tippet or hook length be no longer than twelve inches including all knots, splices or loops. The following diagrams show rigging strategies which comply with these requirements.

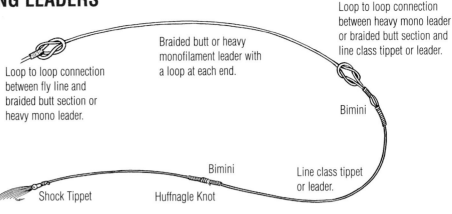

Loop to loop connection between fly line and braided butt section or heavy mono leader.

Braided butt or heavy monofilament leader with a loop at each end.

Loop to loop connection between heavy mono leader or braided butt section and line class tippet or leader.

Bimini

Bimini

Line class tippet or leader.

Shock Tippet

Huffnagle Knot

BIMINI TO HEAVY MONOFILAMENT LEADER (HUFFNAGLE KNOT)

The Huffnagle principle allows a heavy monofilament leader to be tied flush with a double splice, in this case a Bimini, to control the overall length of a shock tippet with no loss of breaking strain to the leader.

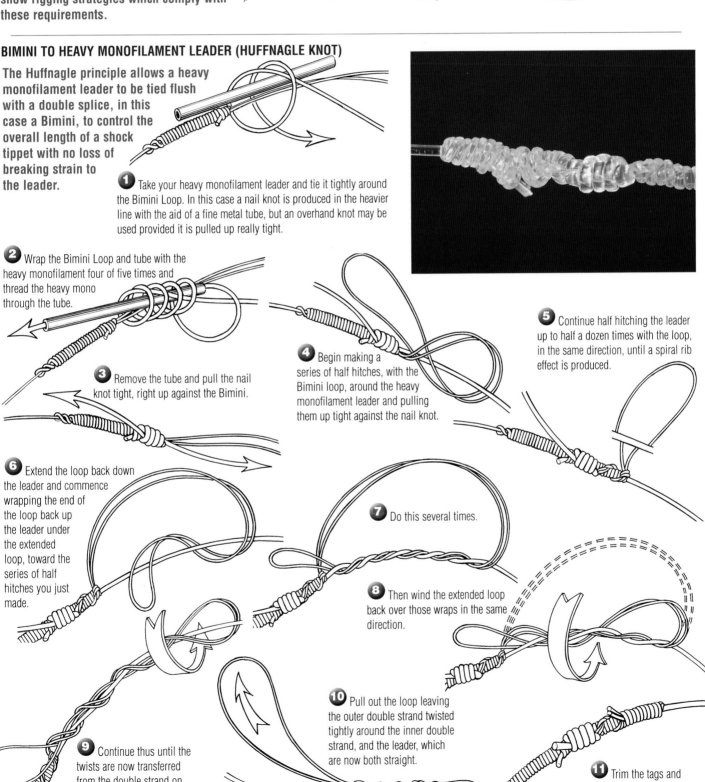

1 Take your heavy monofilament leader and tie it tightly around the Bimini Loop. In this case a nail knot is produced in the heavier line with the aid of a fine metal tube, but an overhand knot may be used provided it is pulled up really tight.

2 Wrap the Bimini Loop and tube with the heavy monofilament four of five times and thread the heavy mono through the tube.

3 Remove the tube and pull the nail knot tight, right up against the Bimini.

4 Begin making a series of half hitches, with the Bimini loop, around the heavy monofilament leader and pulling them up tight against the nail knot.

5 Continue half hitching the leader up to half a dozen times with the loop, in the same direction, until a spiral rib effect is produced.

6 Extend the loop back down the leader and commence wrapping the end of the loop back up the leader under the extended loop, toward the series of half hitches you just made.

7 Do this several times.

8 Then wind the extended loop back over those wraps in the same direction.

9 Continue thus until the twists are now transferred from the double strand on the inside to the double strand on the outside.

10 Pull out the loop leaving the outer double strand twisted tightly around the inner double strand, and the leader, which are now both straight.

11 Trim the tags and the join is complete.

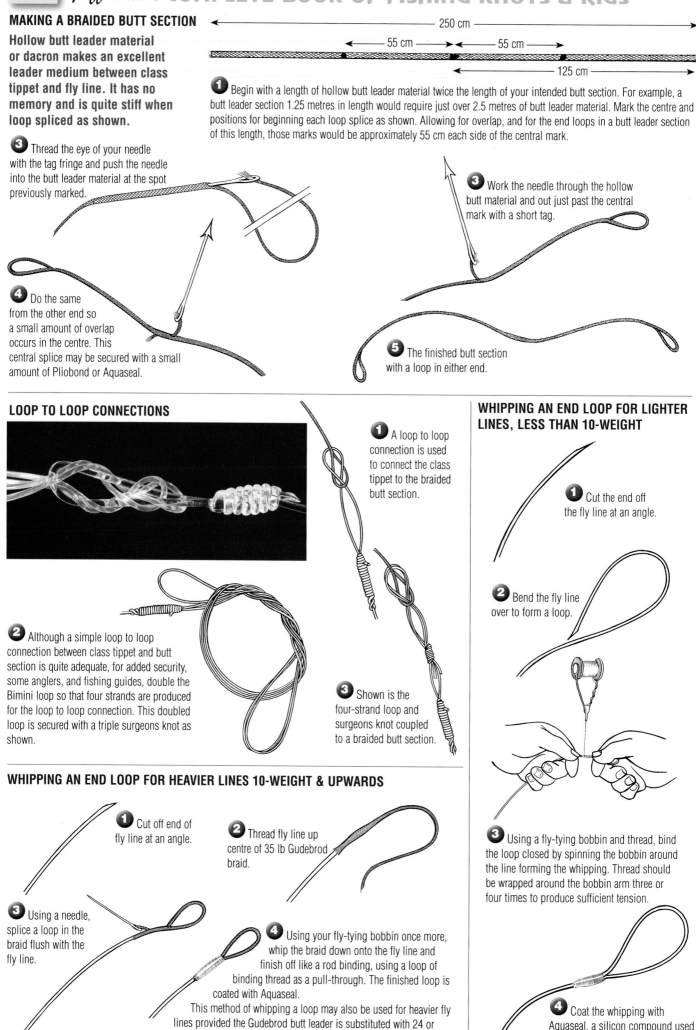

MAKING A BRAIDED BUTT SECTION

Hollow butt leader material or dacron makes an excellent leader medium between class tippet and fly line. It has no memory and is quite stiff when loop spliced as shown.

←———————— 250 cm ————————→

←— 55 cm —→←— 55 cm —→

←—————— 125 cm ——————→

1 Begin with a length of hollow butt leader material twice the length of your intended butt section. For example, a butt leader section 1.25 metres in length would require just over 2.5 metres of butt leader material. Mark the centre and positions for beginning each loop splice as shown. Allowing for overlap, and for the end loops in a butt leader section of this length, those marks would be approximately 55 cm each side of the central mark.

3 Thread the eye of your needle with the tag fringe and push the needle into the butt leader material at the spot previously marked.

3 Work the needle through the hollow butt material and out just past the central mark with a short tag.

4 Do the same from the other end so a small amount of overlap occurs in the centre. This central splice may be secured with a small amount of Pliobond or Aquaseal.

5 The finished butt section with a loop in either end.

LOOP TO LOOP CONNECTIONS

1 A loop to loop connection is used to connect the class tippet to the braided butt section.

2 Although a simple loop to loop connection between class tippet and butt section is quite adequate, for added security, some anglers, and fishing guides, double the Bimini loop so that four strands are produced for the loop to loop connection. This doubled loop is secured with a triple surgeons knot as shown.

3 Shown is the four-strand loop and surgeons knot coupled to a braided butt section.

WHIPPING AN END LOOP FOR LIGHTER LINES, LESS THAN 10-WEIGHT

1 Cut the end off the fly line at an angle.

2 Bend the fly line over to form a loop.

3 Using a fly-tying bobbin and thread, bind the loop closed by spinning the bobbin around the line forming the whipping. Thread should be wrapped around the bobbin arm three or four times to produce sufficient tension.

4 Coat the whipping with Aquaseal, a silicon compound used for rubber repairs.

WHIPPING AN END LOOP FOR HEAVIER LINES 10-WEIGHT & UPWARDS

1 Cut off end of fly line at an angle.

2 Thread fly line up centre of 35 lb Gudebrod braid.

3 Using a needle, splice a loop in the braid flush with the fly line.

4 Using your fly-tying bobbin once more, whip the braid down onto the fly line and finish off like a rod binding, using a loop of binding thread as a pull-through. The finished loop is coated with Aquaseal.

This method of whipping a loop may also be used for heavier fly lines provided the Gudebrod butt leader is substituted with 24 or 37 kg class dacron.

WESTY'S DROPPER

Shown to me by Peter West, this knot allows an additional dropper to be attached to a fly tippet.

1 Make an overhand loop in the tippet.

2 Pull a loop of line through as if to make an indicator knot.

3 Take the dropper line, thread it through the loop, and begin wrapping the standing part with the tag.

4 Having made three or four wraps, thread the tag back through the first wrap so a half blood knot is formed.

5 Tighten both knots in turn; first the half blood knot and then the indicator knot.

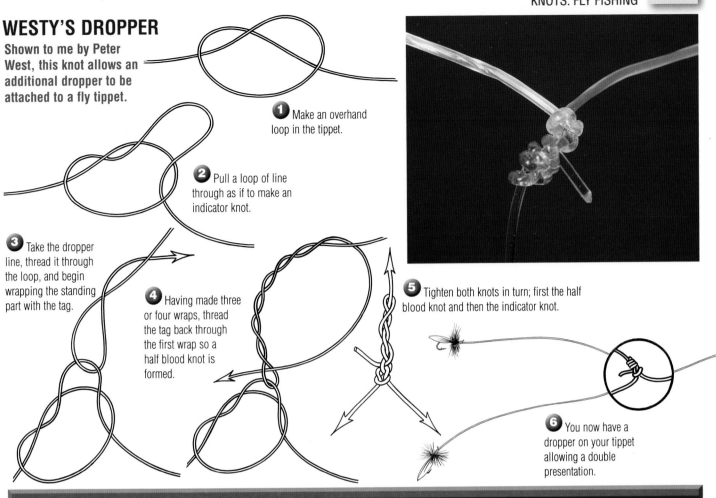

6 You now have a dropper on your tippet allowing a double presentation.

CREATING END LOOPS IN SALTWATER FLY LEADERS

Loop to Loop connections, between leader and flyline, and between leader and class tippet, are frequently used in saltwater flyfishing. When used with heavy monofilament, this procedure allows the angler to control the size of the loop.

1 Make this double loop configuration in the end of your heavy monofilament leader, one loop small, the other large.

2 Wrap the smaller loop with the larger loop.

3 Shown is an effective way of doing this.

4 Having made six or seven wraps, pull the tag to close what is remaining of the large loop.

5 Pass the remaining loop around a fixture with desired diameter to act as a loop gauge, and close the knot, first by pulling firmly on the main or standing part of the leader.

6 Still maintaining some pressure on the standing part, pull gently, but very firmly on the tag until you feel the knot lock the loop in position. Trim the tag.

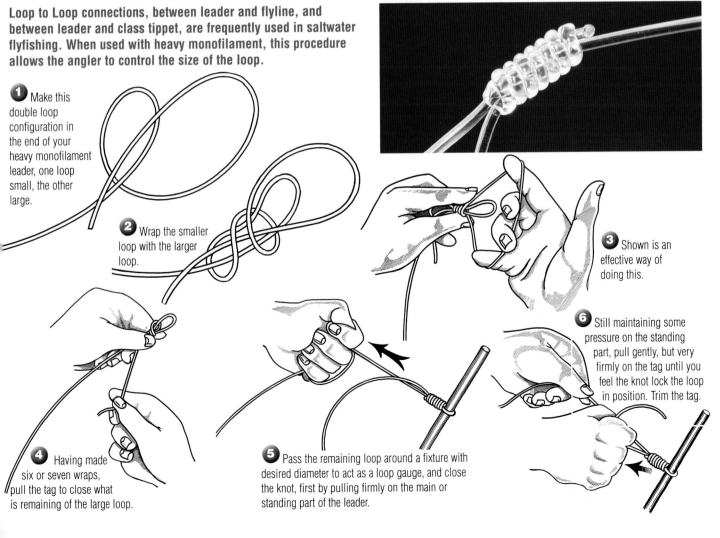

RIGS

The most basic application of a float is to suspend your bait below the surface. Some floats are fixed on the line so the hook remains a constant distance below the float. Others are designed to slide along the line to make casting easier when the bait needs to be presented deeper than usual. There are enough floats, in all types, shapes and sizes, to fill a book. Fortunately, we can get by with just a few. Let's look at some basic floats and ways of fishing with them.

FIXED STEM FLOATS

Stem floats consist of a stem, usually with a pear or cigar-shaped body for added buoyancy. Those stem floats without the body are referred to as pencil floats or quills.

Stem floats used to be made from wooden stems with cork bodies. These days, many are made from plastic. Most have a plastic or rubber sleeve, which fits over the stem at the top to fix the float in position on the line.

1 The first step in rigging with a stem float is to remove the sleeve from the stem and pass the line through it, then through the line guide at the bottom of the stem.

2 When the required amount of line has been passed through sleeve and line guide, slide the sleeve back over the stem to fix the float in position on the line.

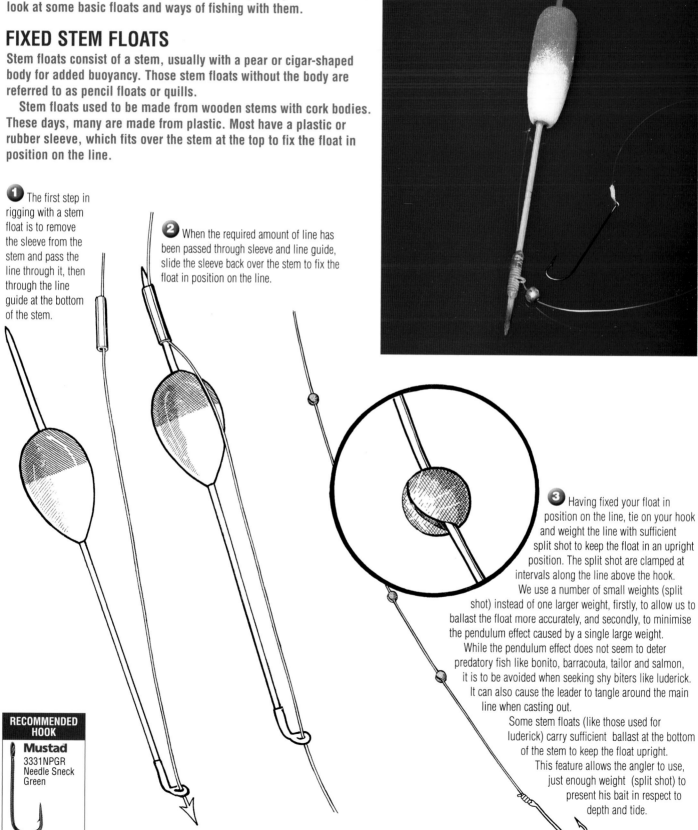

3 Having fixed your float in position on the line, tie on your hook and weight the line with sufficient split shot to keep the float in an upright position. The split shot are clamped at intervals along the line above the hook.

We use a number of small weights (split shot) instead of one larger weight, firstly, to allow us to ballast the float more accurately, and secondly, to minimise the pendulum effect caused by a single large weight.

While the pendulum effect does not seem to deter predatory fish like bonito, barracouta, tailor and salmon, it is to be avoided when seeking shy biters like luderick. It can also cause the leader to tangle around the main line when casting out.

Some stem floats (like those used for luderick) carry sufficient ballast at the bottom of the stem to keep the float upright. This feature allows the angler to use, just enough weight (split shot) to present his bait in respect to depth and tide.

RECOMMENDED HOOK

Mustad
3331NPGR
Needle Sneck
Green

FIXED WAGGLER FLOAT

Wagglers are stem floats, and stem floats can be rigged as wagglers. However floats designed to be rigged as wagglers carry their body (if they have a body), lower on the stem, and the line guide at the bottom of the float is straight.

BOB FLOAT

Bob floats are popular among pier fishermen seeking mullet and garfish. The floats come in several sizes and consist of a plastic sphere, usually red and white, with a spring-loaded catch to fix them onto the line.

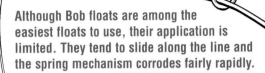

Although Bob floats are among the easiest floats to use, their application is limited. They tend to slide along the line and the spring mechanism corrodes fairly rapidly.

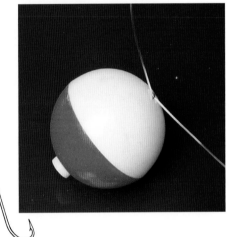

RUNNING FLOATS

Running floats have a hole through the centre, just like a running sinker. We use running floats when we have to present a bait deeper than the length of drop we can cast when using a fixed float.

2 We are now going to fashion that short piece of lumo tube into a float stop.

2a Thread your line through the short length of lumo tube.

2b Measure off the depth at which your bait is to be presented and re-thread the lumo tube as before, taking care not to tie a knot in the line.

2c Close the loop.

2d You will observe that the lumo tube closes tightly on the line at the point determined by yourself.

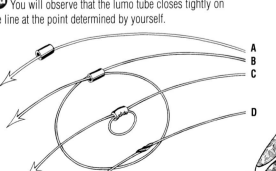

A
B
C

D

1 Shown is a length of lumo tube, some lumo beads and one of those clever Glitter Bird floats with the prismatic decals which flash in the sun. Also shown is a flight of three ganged hooks and a small ball sinker, just heavy enough to keep the float upright in the water. Begin by cutting off a tiny piece of lumo tube, no more than 3 mm in length.

3 Thread on a lumo bead to prevent the stopper from sliding right through the float, then thread on your float.

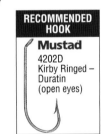

4a Thread on your sinker then tie on your flight of ganged hooks. You will notice that the float sits right on the sinker making it easy for the angler to cast out.

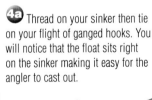

4b When the angler casts out, the baited hooks sink to the depth determined by the position of the lumo stop on the line, whether that depth is two metres or ten metres.

ALTERNATIVE RUNNING FLOAT

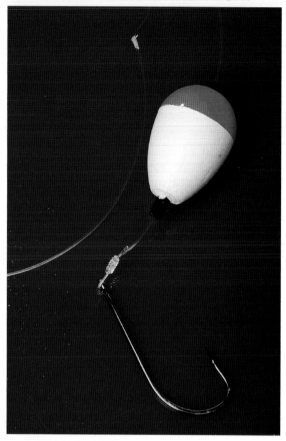

A running float may also be rigged by attaching a leader of heavy line to the lighter main line; say a 30 kg leader to a 10 kg mainline. We do this using the Improved Albright knot I have already described.

This rig is favoured by anglers live baiting from the rocks for pelagic fish such as tuna. You will appreciate that once the leader knot is on the reel, the angler has more control over the fish below. He may even be able to lift smaller fish like bonito straight out onto the rocks without gaffing them.

TANDEM FLOATS

Sometimes we use two floats on the same line, each float serving its specific purpose. Here are two examples.

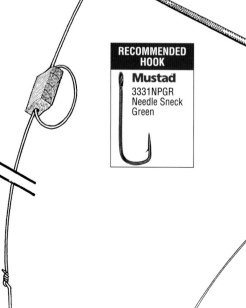

BUBBLE FLOAT

Bubble floats are used by freshwater fishermen fishing in lakes. The bubble float is partially filled with water to make it heavy enough to cast out. This is done by displacing the tube and allowing the water to trickle in.

Bubble floats are made from clear plastic and resemble a bubble. This is probably advantageous because it looks so natural, but the purpose of using clear plastic is to enable the angler to see the amount of water inside the float.

The bubble float is threaded onto the line. A floating stopper is also threaded onto the line and fixed in place to suspend the baited hook at the required depth. In this case, the floating stopper is a small piece of cork through which I have made a hole to thread the line with a red-hot needle. I thread the cork a second time to fix it in place on the line.

When the rig is cast out, both floats lay on the surface side by side. However, when a fish takes the bait, only the small float moves, the larger bubble float remains in place, the fish pulling line through the float with no resistance.

BERLEY CAGE FLOAT

This rig is used for garfish and mullet. The berley float is threaded onto the line and a split shot is clamped onto the line below. This prevents the berley float from sliding off, and determines the depth at which the bait will be presented.

A waggler float is then threaded onto the line and fixed in place with a second split shot as shown. Another split shot is usually added above the hook to make the bait sink.

The berley float is filled with berley to attract the fish while the waggler float serves the dual purpose of fixing the depth of the bait below the surface and indicating bites. Like the bubble float in freshwater fishing, line passes through the berley float without restriction when the bait is taken.

USING BOB FLOATS FOR SMALL FISH

Bob floats are spring loaded plastic spheres. They are favoured by anglers fishing from piers, wharves and jetties. The spring loaded hook simply clamps onto the line at the required depth, and the rig is lowered over the side where it will signal a bite should the bait be taken.

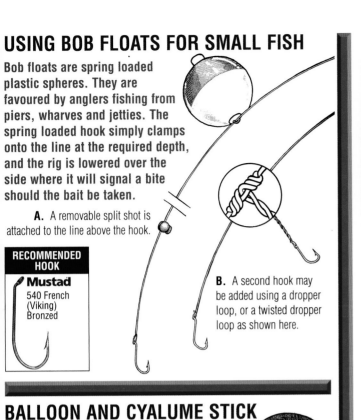

A. A removable split shot is attached to the line above the hook.

B. A second hook may be added using a dropper loop, or a twisted dropper loop as shown here.

RECOMMENDED HOOK

Mustad
540 French (Viking) Bronzed

BALLOON AND CYALUME STICK

Balloon with cyalume or light inside tied to a loop of line for night fishing. Note that the lip of the balloon has been removed so that it does not catch in the loop when a fish takes the bait and pulls the line tight. For maximum light emission, cyalumes should match balloon colour as closely as possible.

BERLEY FLOATS

Berley floats may be rigged as running floats like this one, which is rigged to run between a top stopper and a heavy split shot. Both hooks are rigged below the split shot, one tied to the end of the line, the other rigged on a dropper loop.

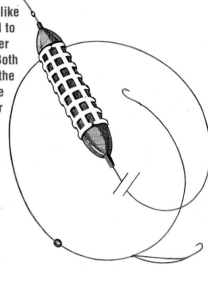

RECOMMENDED HOOK

Mustad
4202D Kirby Ringed – Duratin (open eyes)

FLOAT-FISHING FOR BOTTOM FEEDERS

While most bottom feeders are taken on baits weighted with sinkers on the bottom, in situations where there is a heavy weed growth, or other bottom obstructions, suspending a bait just above the bottom is more productive. Let's look at how to do that both in shallow water, and the deep.

1. Shallow Water

A. When fishing shallow water, the float is fixed in place with a silicone band because the entire rig can be cast quite easily.

B. Large split shot, sufficient to ballast the float with just the tip showing, are clamped onto the line beneath the float.

C. A tiny split shot is clamped onto the line about 7 cm (nearly 3") above the hook to provide sufficient tension for even the lightest of bites to be felt.

D. For night fishing a light stick is secured to the tip of the float using a length of silicone rubber tubing.

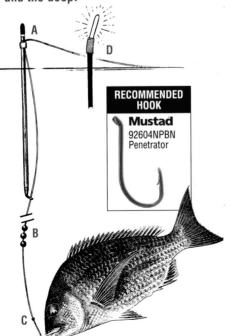

RECOMMENDED HOOK

Mustad
92604NPBN Penetrator

2. Deep Water

A. When fishing deep water, the float must slide along the line so a stopper is placed in the line at the required depth. I use a tiny piece (about 2 mm) of Lumo tube through which the line is passed twice and then pulled tight.

B. Next a Lumo bead is threaded onto the line to prevent the float adapter from riding over the stopper.

C. The float, or float adapter (to allow floats to be changed), is threaded onto the line so it can slide.

D. A second Lumo bead is threaded onto the line so that the float adapter does not jam on the swivel.

E. A small (number 10) swivel.

F. Clamp sufficient split shot on the line to ballast the float.

G. A tiny shot is clamped onto the line about 7 cm (nearly 3") above the hook to provide sufficient tension for even the lightest of bites to be felt.

RECOMMENDED HOOK

Mustad
32813NPBLM Fine Worm

ATTACHING BALLOONS

Large balloons, like the Ansell 60 to 80 gram models are reusable provided they can be removed from the towline without damage. Here is a useful method of attaching large balloons to a towline so that they can be removed without damage.

All you will need is a short piece of clear plastic tube with an approximate 10 mm inside diameter, about 50 mm long and some very heavy monofilament, say 100 kg breaking strain or so. You can use garden hose, but it is heavy and may impede the balloon in a downdraft.

1 Thread the heavy mono through the 50 mm length of plastic tubing.

2 Make a noose in your heavy mono. Recommended is the Centauri knot but with only two wraps.

3 Tie a simple loop in the other end of the mono, either a blood bight or a double overhand loop will do.

4 Place the noose over the neck of the balloon, then place the balloon over the filling nozzle on the gas cylinder and pull the noose tight. Fill the balloon with gas and remove it from the nozzle.

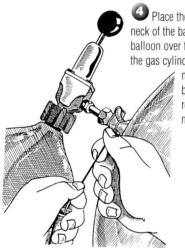

5 Holding the tube in one hand, pull the neck of the balloon into the tube with the other. It will stay in place and be easy to remove when you have finished fishing.

6 Attach your balloon by tying the towline to the loop in the heavy monofilament. Recommended for this purpose is the Centauri knot shown.

TOWLINE KNOT

Helium filled balloons are useful for taking out baits from the rocks or other land based locations when the wind is blowing offshore.

The most effective strategy is to tie the balloon to a towline, and—only when the balloon has reached the true air current—is the towline tied to the leader. However, should a hooked fish not free the towline, it may tangle in the line, and—in a worse case scenario—prevent the angler from winding the line back onto his reel before the fish can be brought within gaffing range.

To overcome this problem I use a special knot called a towline knot. The towline knot will not slip while the balloon is towing out the bait, but when a fish becomes hooked and strain is placed on the line, the towline just pops off.

These are the steps in tying a towline knot.

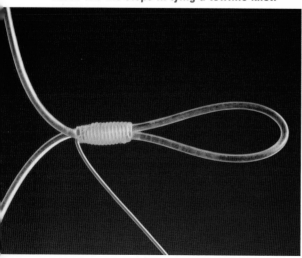

1 Make a loop in the leader and make a loop in the end of the towline alongside.

2 Wrap the loop in the towline around the loop in the leader, and the towline tag, just like you were snelling a hook onto your line.

3 Continue until you have made a dozen or so wraps.

4 Then close the knot down hard on the loop in your leader and trim the tag.

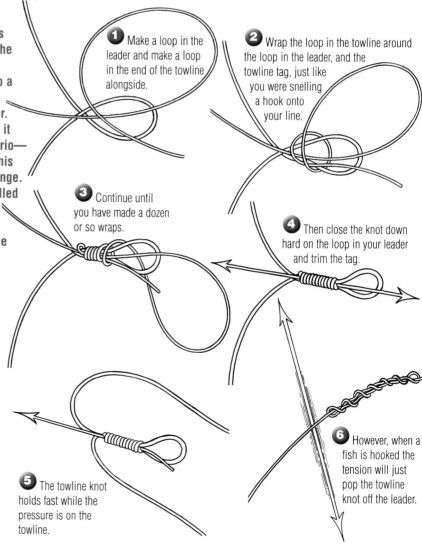

5 The towline knot holds fast while the pressure is on the towline.

6 However, when a fish is hooked the tension will just pop the towline knot off the leader.

RIGS

FISHING WITH SINKERS: FIXED SINKER RIGS

Paternoster, or Fixed Sinker Rig, using Locked Half Blood Knot for all connections. A preferred option when rigging for maximum strength such as in surf casting.

Paternoster, or Fixed Sinker Rig, using loop connections for convenience and speed. The hooks are attached using Twisted Dropper Loops so that they stand away from the main line and don't tangle.

RECOMMENDED HOOK
Mustad
92553NPBN
Octopus Hook

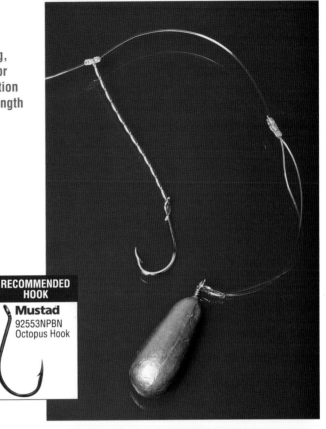

FISHING WITH SINKERS: RUNNING SINKER RIGS

1 Shown is the simplest of all running sinker rigs with the sinker running all of the way down to the hook. Although simple and effective, this rig has its limitations. Firstly, the sinker can't be too large because it may crush any of the bait threaded up the line above the hook. Secondly, no provision can be made for using a heavier leader to the hook, a desirable feature when seeking large fish like mulloway and big snapper.

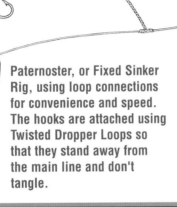

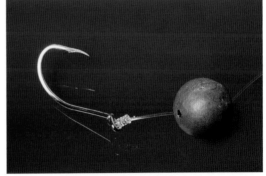

2 Shown is a more complex running sinker rig featuring two hooks on a separate leader one sliding along the leader and one tied on the end. At the other end of the leader is a solid metal ring to which the hook leader is tied, the knot shown in both cases is a blood knot.

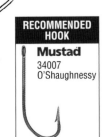

RECOMMENDED HOOK
Mustad
34007
O'Shaughnessy

3 Shown is the Ezy Rig which slides along the line like a running sinker. It allows a bomb sinker, which would normally be tied on the end of the line, to be used as a running sinker.

It consists of a plastic barrel, which slides along the line, to which is attached a metal snap for changing sinkers as required.

FISHING WITH SINKERS: TANGLE-FREE SURF-CASTING RIG

To build this rig you will need to have a bomb-style sinker with a hook on it instead of an eye or ring.

Over several tests with two different anglers and sets of tackle, the improvement in distance when using this rig, over the conventional rig with the baited hook unsecured, varied from 10% (73 to 81 metres), to 25% (88 to 110 metres). However, not only was casting distance increased but the tendency for the overhead reels used to overrun, was reduced.

3 Attach the bait securely but with the hook right at the bottom. Shown is a pilchard attached with Bait Mate, an elastic thread that is available from leading fishing tackle shops and used for this very purpose. Note also in this diagram that I've introduced an alternative method of rigging with two solid brass rings to form a running sinker, an option preferred by some anglers.

1a You can make up a suitable sinker with the addition of a fishhook from which the point has been removed, and the eye opened so it can be fitted to the eye of the swivel on the sinker before being closed again. I use Mustad 8260 Limericks in size 4/0 and find them excellent.

1b However, it may be more satisfactory to make up sinkers especially with a stout wire hook, or a fishhook with the point and barb cut off, moulded into the sinker.

4 The bait should be rigged with the hook right at the end. I use hosiery elastic, sold in leading tackle stores under the brand name of Bait Mate, to secure the bait to the hook in the manner shown. Having baited your hook, engage the hook on the sinker so the hook leader now supports the weight of your sinker. The sinker lead, which is longer than the hook lead, will now be slack of course.

2 Note how the rig is built using a solid brass ring to which the leader is tied. Also, note particularly that the lead from the ring to the sinker is longer than the lead from the ring to the hook. This difference is vital to the function of the rig.

RECOMMENDED HOOK

Mustad
92553NPBN
Octopus Hook

5 The baited hook remains engaged with the sinker throughout the cast, preventing the bait from flapping around and tangling in your main line. However, when the sinker hits the water, the baited hook disengages from the sinker. A couple of practise casts should convince you of this.

BAITING UP: SOFT BAITS

To cover every conceivable bait and its best presentation is beyond the scope of this series. However, on the next few pages we will look at a few examples of different baits commonly used in salt water and effective ways of presenting them.

Soft baits like tuna flesh and craytail are among the most attractive baits to saltwater fish. Unfortunately they often fly off the hook when the line is cast out. The best method of securing soft baits to the hook is with hosiery elastic. Hosiery elastic is sold in leading fishing tackle stores on special plastic spools for this purpose under the brand name "Bait Mate".

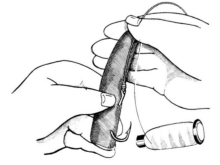

1 Take a strip of tuna flesh (it need not have any skin on it) insert your hook as previously shown, then lay the leader alongside the strip.

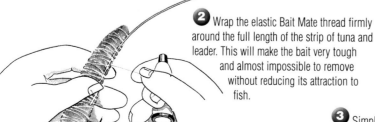

2 Wrap the elastic Bait Mate thread firmly around the full length of the strip of tuna and leader. This will make the bait very tough and almost impossible to remove without reducing its attraction to fish.

3 Simply snap off the Bait Mate thread and it sticks like the proverbial: There is no need to tie knots in it.

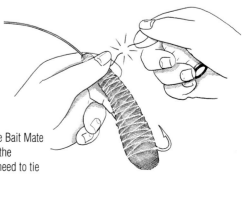

MAKING A FLEXIBLE FLIGHT OF GANGED HOOKS

A flight of ganged hooks may be made longer and more flexible by joining them with suitable size swivels.

You can make them in any size but I used size 4/0 hooks and No 4 swivels as models for this set of illustrations.

I also used 4 mm vinyl tubing which you can buy at a haberdashery, but you can use heat-shrink tubing as an alternative.

1 Cut the tubing into short lengths that will fit over the eyes of your swivels.

2 The point of the hook goes through the tubing on the swivel while the open eye of the hook goes through the other end.

RECOMMENDED HOOK

Mustad
4202D
Kirby Ringed –
Duratin
(open eyes)

3 The gang can be made with two, three or more hooks, the eye of each hook being closed to secure the gang.

DROP-SHOT RIG

Shown is a method of rigging a soft plastic lure on a hook perpendicular to the main line. Materials required are:

- Two small plastic beads.
- A suitable straight hook with a fairly large eye.
- A soft plastic lure body of suitable size.

1 Cut the main line at the point the lure is to be attached and thread one end through the hook and two beads in the order shown.

2 Thread the hook and two beads with the other end of the main line but in the opposite direction.

3 Tie a uni-knot first below the threaded sequence.

4 Then above with the other line.

5 Close the uni-knots together and thread the soft plastic onto the hook.

RECOMMENDED HOOK

Mustad
32813NPBLM
Fine Worm

6 When a sinker is attached, the lure should be perpendicular to the line.

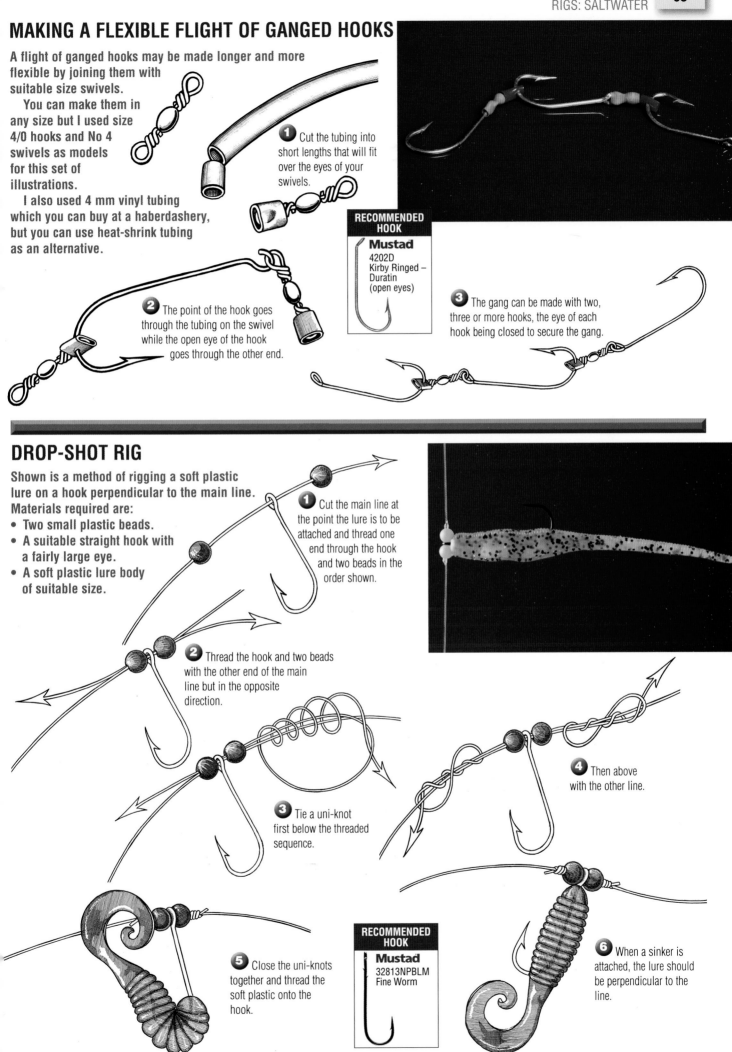

PATERNOSTER RIG

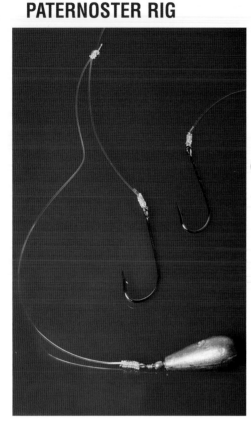

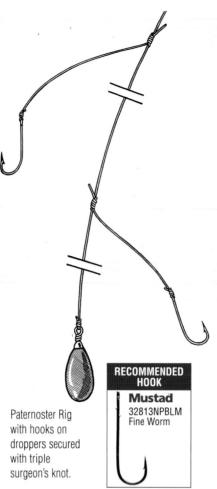

Paternoster Rig with hooks on droppers secured with triple surgeon's knot.

RECOMMENDED HOOK

Mustad
32813NPBLM
Fine Worm

ROUGH BOTTOM RIG

RECOMMENDED HOOK

Mustad
92554NPNR
Big Red

RECOMMENDED HOOK

Mustad
92553NPBN
Octopus Hook

A. Big splash water bomb balloon inflated to thumbnail size to buoy bait up from bottom.

B. Bait rigged on two hooks and secured with hosiery elastic (Bait Mate).

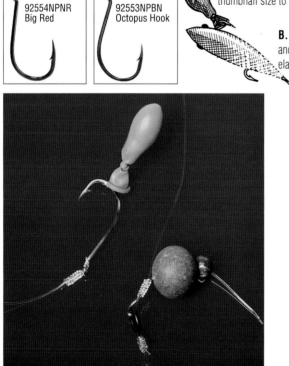

C. Solid metal ring or swivel.

D. Ball sinker threaded on knot tag from main line.

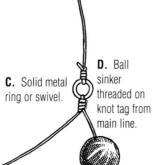

F. Main line to rod and reel.

E. Removable split shot clamped onto knot tag to hold sinker in place.

DEPLOYING LARGE BAITS FROM THE BEACH

Casting out a large bait from a surf beach, for sharks and other large fish, has always been difficult. However, the 'Uni-directional sliding clip', supplied by Ranger Camping, 08 9444 9633, email: joe@rangercamping.com.au, solves that problem.

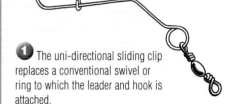

1 The uni-directional sliding clip replaces a conventional swivel or ring to which the leader and hook is attached.

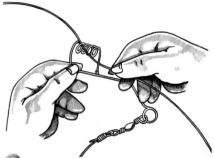

2 Having cast a large sinker out past the breaker line, the clip is undone and the spiral section wound onto the line, then secured so it slides freely.

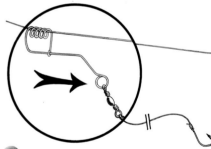

3 On a tight line, the wave action will take clip, leader and baited hook, all the way out to the sinker which may be 100 metres (110 yards) or more offshore.

4 Whenever an incoming wave catches the baited hook and pulls it back, the Uni-directional clip simply turns around, taking an angle bite on the line so that it cannot be washed back. When the wave recedes, the clip assumes its original position and goes out once more.

BAITING UP: CRUSTACEANS

Crustacean baits are high on the desired list of fish from bonefish to salmon.

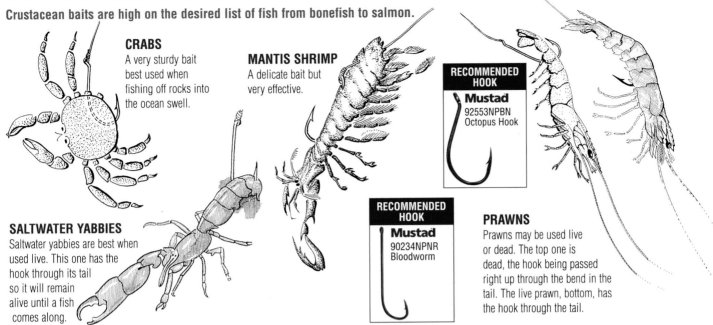

CRABS
A very sturdy bait best used when fishing off rocks into the ocean swell.

MANTIS SHRIMP
A delicate bait but very effective.

RECOMMENDED HOOK
Mustad
92553NPBN
Octopus Hook

SALTWATER YABBIES
Saltwater yabbies are best when used live. This one has the hook through its tail so it will remain alive until a fish comes along.

RECOMMENDED HOOK
Mustad
90234NPNR
Bloodworm

PRAWNS
Prawns may be used live or dead. The top one is dead, the hook being passed right up through the bend in the tail. The live prawn, bottom, has the hook through the tail.

BAITING UP: MOLLUSCS

Mussels and pipis etc, are best bound to the hook with Bait Mate, like other soft baits when casting out in the surf.

However when casting requirements are modest, and quick bait changes are required, a different approach is suggested.

By alternately passing the hook through the bait, then winding the bait back around the hook, the bait is gradually worked up the shank of the hook. This is just a bit slower than just hooking the bait on in one go, but you catch more fish in the long run because presentation is better and fish find it harder to get off the hook.

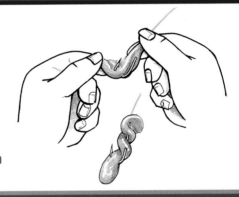

BAITING UP: COMMON SALTWATER BAITS

When baiting a hook the bait should be secure, and the point of the hook should be sufficiently exposed to hook the fish. Only when using live bait is security compromised to some extent to keep the bait alive.

Fishing with natural, fresh, or live bait on a carefully selected hook is the most effective way of catching fish on a fishing line. The baits and baiting methods in this chapter are by no means comprehensive, but they do represent a good cross section of what is used. Here are some more.

WEED
Adapting a standard up or down-turned eye hook into a bait holder hook.

1 By tying a simple Improved Snell or a Snell formed down on the shank of the hook, you will have a ready-made loop to which part of your bait can be inserted.

RECOMMENDED HOOK
Mustad
3331NPGR
Needle Sneck Green

2 In this case weed is inserted through the loop and wound down the shank of the hook. Bait is secured with a tie around the curve of the hook.

CLAMS
The soft shelled clam (squirter) is easily baited up by inserting the hook adjacent to it's hinge. Push the hook right through using an implement such as a barbeque skewer. Then pull the hook back so that the spear overlaps shell.

RECOMMENDED HOOK
Mustad
92604NPBN
Penetrator

MAGGOTS
Blowfly maggots are used in fresh water for a wide variety of fish, but will take saltwater species like garfish, bream and whiting to name just a few.

Maggots are hooked in the tail (large) end on a small hook say size 12 down to 16. They may be used singly or several at a time.

WORMS
Worms may be threaded on a hook singly or in pieces and bunched using several at a time.

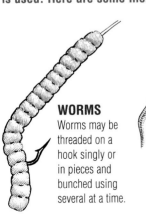
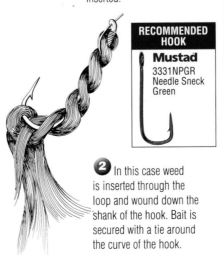

BAITING UP AND FISHING WITH TUNA CIRCLES

Tuna circles are fish hooks which differ from conventional hooks in that the point of the hook faces back toward the shank at something approaching a right angle.

The tuna circle is designed to trap any ridge of cartilage, bone, gill-arch, lip, tongue, jaw hinge etc, in the gap between the point of the hook and the shank, a situation once initiated is almost impossible to reverse, hence their effectiveness.

Tuna circles have long been used by commercial long-liners, particularly for large pelagic fish like tuna, but they work equally well on all species from broadbill to bream.

They are especially effective in game and sportfishing situations where the fish may take a long time—sometimes hours—to bring in. This is because, once they are in place, tuna circles are very difficult to dislodge.

They are also particularly effective in bottom bouncing in the deep sea where any fish, once hooked, must be brought up a very long way, sometimes several hundred metres. Tuna circles save the disappointment many deep sea anglers experience on battling a really heavy blue eye trevalla, trumpeter or whatever, only to lose it when the hook tears out just as it is nearing the boat.

Anglers rarely use tuna circles because they must be baited correctly or they will not work.

This article details some deadly methods of baiting with tuna circles. Let's see how the job is done.

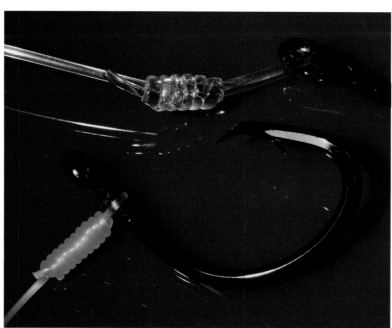

STRIP BAITING WITH TUNA CIRCLES

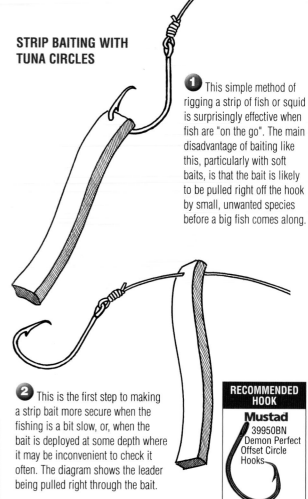

1 This simple method of rigging a strip of fish or squid is surprisingly effective when fish are "on the go". The main disadvantage of baiting like this, particularly with soft baits, is that the bait is likely to be pulled right off the hook by small, unwanted species before a big fish comes along.

2 This is the first step to making a strip bait more secure when the fishing is a bit slow, or, when the bait is deployed at some depth where it may be inconvenient to check it often. The diagram shows the leader being pulled right through the bait.

RECOMMENDED HOOK

Mustad
39950BN
Demon Perfect
Offset Circle
Hooks

3 Next we fold the strip and impale the fold with the point of the hook. Not too deep mind you because we don't want to obstruct the gap between the point and the shank. If we do this, then the hook becomes ineffective.

4 This is a more secure bait presentation. However, some anglers may be deterred by seeing how proud the hook sits out from the bait. But that is a situation which can be easily remedied.

5 The first step in making the hook appear less conspicuous is to cut the strip off below the hook.

6 Fold the cut section over tightly and impale the fold.

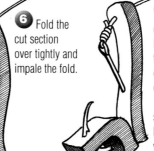

7 Push the folded strip down into the curve of the hook. This is a very effective bait presentation which substantially hides the hook without reducing its efficacy. Its disadvantage is that the bait is inclined to spin on the retrieve or when fished in a current.

The spinning bait problem is substantially solved in deep sea presentations when the hook is rigged on a twisted dropper loop which is far less inclined to spin and tangle around the main line.

RIGGING CIRCLES ON HEAVY LEADERS

Circles are most effective when rigged on leaders that are heavy enough to influence the lay of the hook. This entails having the leader protrude forward from the eye so the hook cocks out on an angle to the line. Shown is one way of doing this using a Mustad 39960 circle on heavy monofilament.

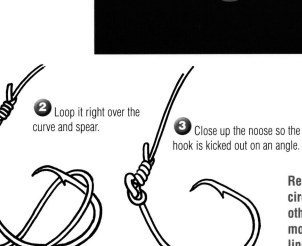

1 Select a leader no lighter than 23 kg (50 pounds) breaking strain and tie a noose or sliding loop in the leader (a Nail Knot with a loop is probably best, but a Uni Knot or Centauri Knot will suffice). Thread the loop through the eye from the front.

2 Loop it right over the curve and spear.

3 Close up the noose so the hook is kicked out on an angle.

RECOMMENDED HOOK

Mustad 39950BN Demon Perfect Offset Circle Hooks

Remember, this method of attaching circles should not be used with any other leader than relatively heavy monofilament, or wire, otherwise line damage may occur from the eye of the hook.

RIGGING CIRCLES ON CABLE

Circle hooks, like the Mustad 39960, may be rigged on 7 strand or 49 strand cable to great effect on sharks and other game fish.

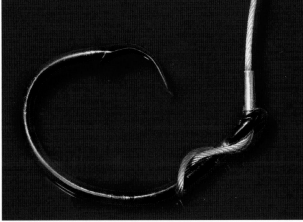

1 Thread the cable through a suitable size metal sleeve, then through the eye of the hook from the front.

RECOMMENDED HOOK

Mustad 39950BN Demon Perfect Offset Circle Hooks

2 Loop the cable around the front of the shank, back through the eye of the hook and then through the sleeve.

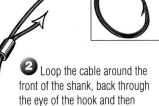

3 Extend the loop of cable, put in a half twist, and loop it over the point of the hook.

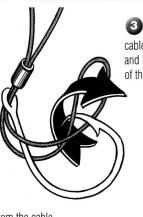

4 Take up the loop, slide the sleeve right up the hook, then — using a set of crimping pliers — crimp the sleeve firmly so the cable cannot slip.

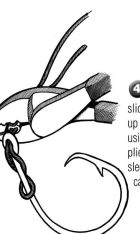

5 Trim the tag from the cable and the hook is secure, but kicked out at a sharp angle to the cable.

6 The bait, in this case a fish fillet, is secured to the leader using electrical cable ties, taking care that the hook remains kicked out from the bait at an angle.

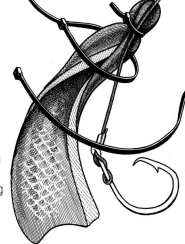

DOUBLE PINCH METHOD OF STRIP BAITING CIRCLES RIGGED ON HEAVY LEADER

When baiting strips of squid or fish on circle hooks, care needs to be taken not to obscure the gap between the point and the shank. The double pinch method of baiting strip baits on circles meets that requirement.

1 Pinch the strip at one end and push the hook over, and through the bend.

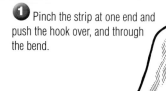

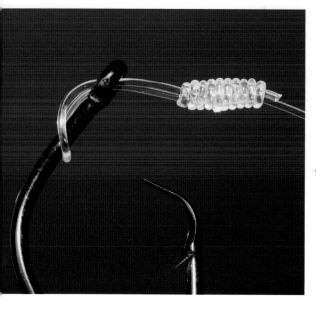

2 Shown is the bait so far, which is quite effective.

RECOMMENDED HOOK

Mustad
39950BN
Demon Perfect
Offset Circle
Hooks

3 For added security a second pinch is made just over a hook length from the first and the same procedure is followed.

4 This bait is not only more effective, but more secure.

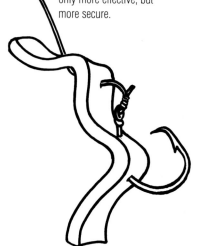

5 The bait may be made more attractive by first, trimming the ends off the strip.

6 Then impaling those ends on the hook.

BAITING CIRCLES RIGGED ON HEAVY LEADERS WITH A SMALL BAITFISH

2 Bind the leader firmly to the bait, taking care not to wrap the hook, then break the thread. The hook should remain clear of the bait as shown in the drawing.

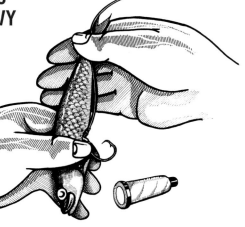

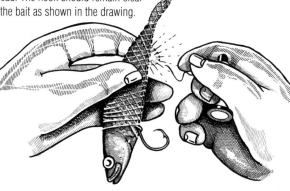

1 Lay the leader alongside a small baitfish like a pilchard so it can be bound to the leader with hosiery elastic (Bait Mate).

BAITING SQUID HEADS ON CIRCLES

Squid and cuttlefish heads are highly regarded as big fish baits. They are most effective when rigged on circle hooks as shown. You need a 30 cm length of strong elastic or rubber, like that from shock cord, a baiting needle and a size 6/0–10/0 circle hook, depending on the size of the head to be baited.

RECOMMENDED HOOK

Mustad
39950BN
Demon Perfect
Offset Circle
Hooks

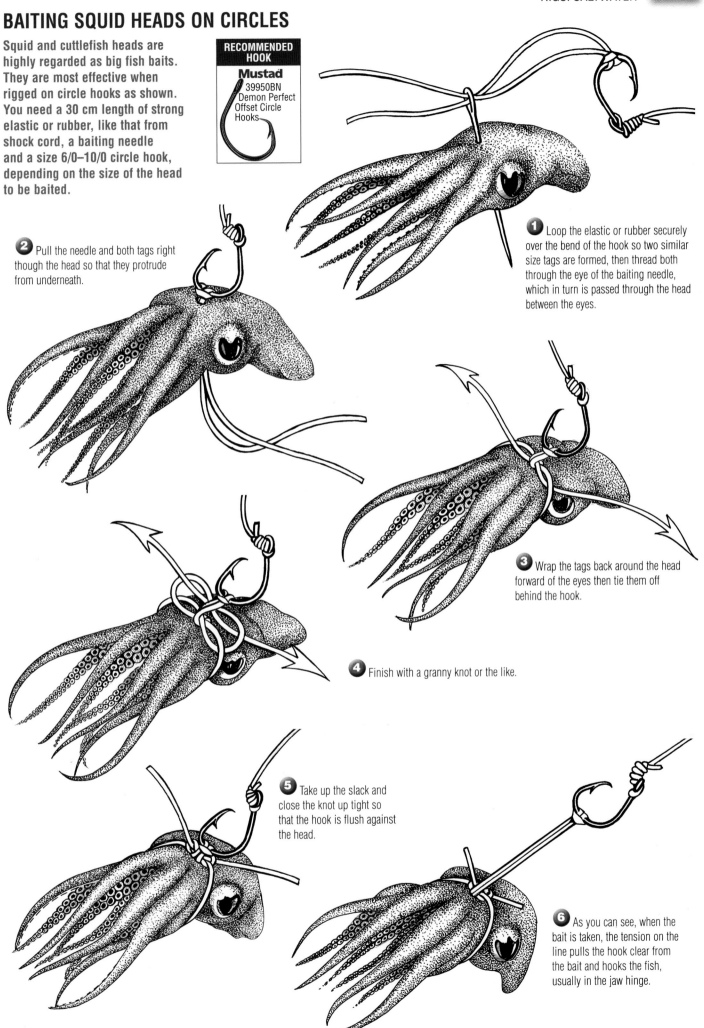

1 Loop the elastic or rubber securely over the bend of the hook so two similar size tags are formed, then thread both through the eye of the baiting needle, which in turn is passed through the head between the eyes.

2 Pull the needle and both tags right though the head so that they protrude from underneath.

3 Wrap the tags back around the head forward of the eyes then tie them off behind the hook.

4 Finish with a granny knot or the like.

5 Take up the slack and close the knot up tight so that the hook is flush against the head.

6 As you can see, when the bait is taken, the tension on the line pulls the hook clear from the bait and hooks the fish, usually in the jaw hinge.

RIGGING FISH HEADS ON CIRCLES FOR SNAPPER

This deadly baiting technique for fish heads makes use of a circle hook, in this case a size 6/0 Mustad Fine Wire Demon (39952), to which is attached a length of hat elastic, available from any haberdashery. Also required is a baiting needle, or what I usually use, a looped length of Galvanised tie wire.

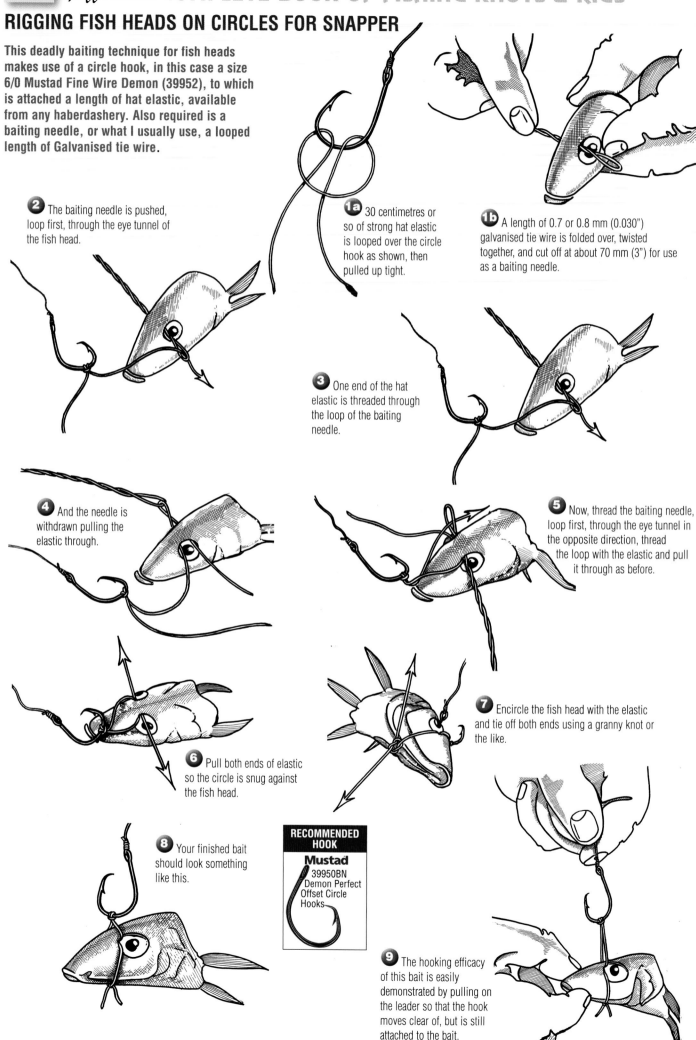

2 The baiting needle is pushed, loop first, through the eye tunnel of the fish head.

1a 30 centimetres or so of strong hat elastic is looped over the circle hook as shown, then pulled up tight.

1b A length of 0.7 or 0.8 mm (0.030") galvanised tie wire is folded over, twisted together, and cut off at about 70 mm (3") for use as a baiting needle.

3 One end of the hat elastic is threaded through the loop of the baiting needle.

4 And the needle is withdrawn pulling the elastic through.

5 Now, thread the baiting needle, loop first, through the eye tunnel in the opposite direction, thread the loop with the elastic and pull it through as before.

6 Pull both ends of elastic so the circle is snug against the fish head.

7 Encircle the fish head with the elastic and tie off both ends using a granny knot or the like.

8 Your finished bait should look something like this.

RECOMMENDED HOOK

Mustad
39950BN
Demon Perfect
Offset Circle
Hooks

9 The hooking efficacy of this bait is easily demonstrated by pulling on the leader so that the hook moves clear of, but is still attached to the bait.

BAITING TUNA CIRCLES WITH LIVE BAITS

Tuna circles are probably the best live baiting hooks ever designed.
This is how to bait them.

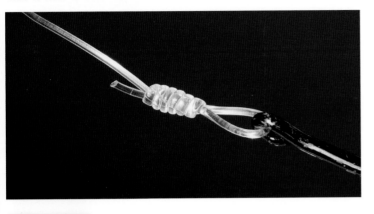

1 Impale the bait fish sideways through the nose.

2 This is the finished bait. Note particularly that the gap between the point and the shank is not obstructed.

BAITING TUNA CIRCLES WITH SOFT BAITS

Tuna flesh without any skin on it, a handful of pipis, mussels oysters, pieces of cray-tail and bait fish like slimy mackerel and pilchards which have been frozen then thawed out again are soft baits.

We attach these soft baits to tuna circle hooks using hosiery elastic which is sold in fishing tackle outlets as Bait Mate. Here is how we bait up with a pilchard. A slimy mackerel requires the same treatment.

1 Drive the point into the bait just behind the breast bone, but not too deep. Then push it forward and bring it back out again.

2 Lay the leader alongside the bait with a strand of Bait Mate, preparatory to commencing a binding down the bait from the tail wrist.

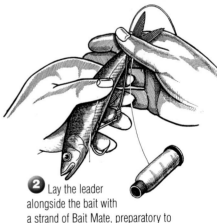

3 Bind the bait tightly all the way down to the hook.

4 Then bind it all the way back again, continuing right past the tail, then back to the tail wrist before snapping the elastic so that it bites into the bait and will not come undone. These baiting methods ensure excellent results with conventional hooks as well, but they are particularly suited to tuna circles because they do not obstruct the gap between the point and the shank.

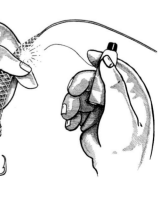

FISH HEAD ON TWO HOOKS

When pickers and lice are on the job, flesh baits do not last very long. That is why fish heads, like this small barracouta head, are preferred when seeking large fish like snapper which may take their time in coming along.

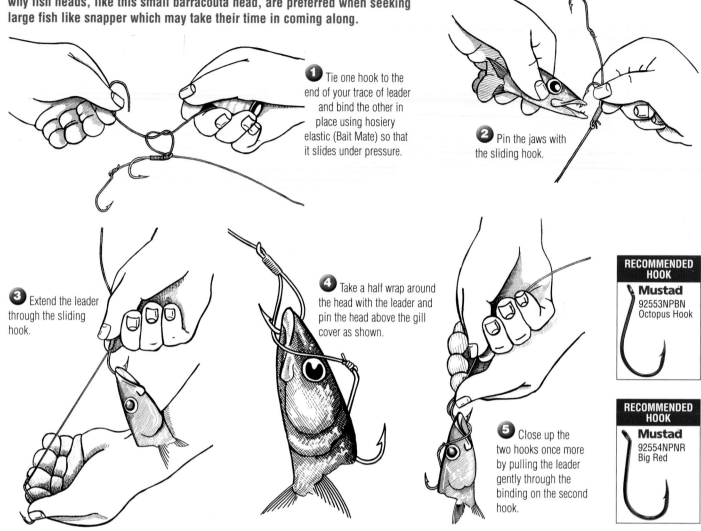

1 Tie one hook to the end of your trace of leader and bind the other in place using hosiery elastic (Bait Mate) so that it slides under pressure.

2 Pin the jaws with the sliding hook.

3 Extend the leader through the sliding hook.

4 Take a half wrap around the head with the leader and pin the head above the gill cover as shown.

5 Close up the two hooks once more by pulling the leader gently through the binding on the second hook.

RECOMMENDED HOOK
Mustad
92553NPBN
Octopus Hook

RECOMMENDED HOOK
Mustad
92554NPNR
Big Red

PUNCHY BARNARD BAIT RIG

This effective bait rig was shown to me by renowned angler Glenn Mitchell and is one of his favourites for big snapper and mulloway. You need a small fish; anything from a large pilchard to a mullet, or perhaps a small but legal size Australian salmon. Hooks size will be from 6/0 to 9/0 in a beak, suicide, or octopus pattern depending on the size of the fish being used for bait.

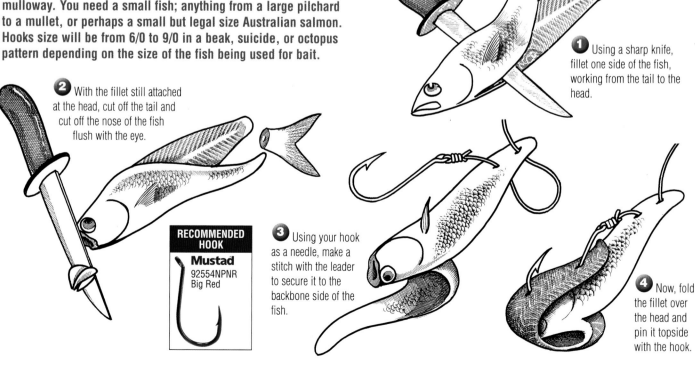

1 Using a sharp knife, fillet one side of the fish, working from the tail to the head.

2 With the fillet still attached at the head, cut off the tail and cut off the nose of the fish flush with the eye.

3 Using your hook as a needle, make a stitch with the leader to secure it to the backbone side of the fish.

4 Now, fold the fillet over the head and pin it topside with the hook.

RECOMMENDED HOOK
Mustad
92554NPNR
Big Red

RIGGING WITH WIRE: FLEMISH EYE

The Flemish Eye is used to attach hooks, rings and swivels to seven and forty-nine strand wire when sport and game fishing. The Flemish Eye is secured with a sleeve, which is firmly crimped with a special pair of pliers called a crimping tool.

1. First slide a sleeve of the correct size over the wire you are using. The size of sleeve required is specified on the packaging of the wire. Sleeves may also be supplied with the wire.

RECOMMENDED HOOK
Mustad
10827NPBLN
Hoodlum

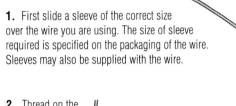

2. Thread on the hook and make an overhand knot in the wire on the eye of the hook.

3. Add one more wrap so that you have an overhand knot with two wraps, not one.

4. Thread the tag through the sleeve alongside the standing part.

5. Slide the Flemish Eye up tight on the eye of the hook, slide the sleeve right up against that, then crimp the sleeve with the crimping tool.

6. Trim off the tag and your hook is secure. Or, an alternative is to leave a short tag which is taped to the standing part to avoid injury from wire splinters.

Multiple Hook Rigs: Double Rigging on Wire

Two-hook rigs are used in game fishing, particularly when trolling lures. This rig, which consists of two hooks, a swivel, a length of multi-strand wire and crimped sleeves, is assembled using a series of Flemish Eyes, a configuration described above.

RECOMMENDED HOOK
Mustad
10827NPBLN
Hoodlum

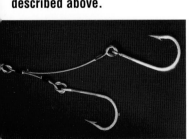

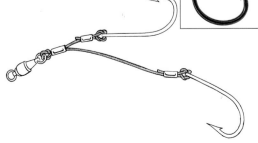

MULTIPLE HOOK RIGS: GANGED HOOKS

Hooks may be ganged together by opening up the eyes on all hooks following the leader hook, passing the point and barb of the preceding hook through, then closing the eye with a pair of pliers.

Never crush the barb of the hook down to facilitate ganging, because although this is sometimes done it is a flawed strategy and has cost many an angler a good fish.

RECOMMENDED HOOK
Mustad
4202D
Kirby Ringed –
Duratin
(open eyes)

1 Some hooks like the Mustad 4202 are packed for sale with the eyes open for ganging.

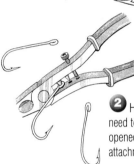

2 However, most hooks need to have the eyes opened with the special cone attachment on fishing pliers.

3 Usually the flight of ganged hooks is attached directly to the end of the anglers line and baited with a small fish.

4 Sometimes, however, a flight of ganged hooks is used when bottom fishing. In this case, a flight of three ganged hooks has been attached to a short, twisted dropper loop (described earlier in this book) so they won't tangle around the main line when "deep-dropping."

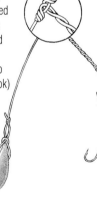

5 Sometimes hooks are linked together using small swivels; just big enough to be threaded over the wire of the hook.

6 This extends the length of the gang and gives it more flexibility. Electrolysis may become a problem with this method following extended use.

MAKING A BAIT NEEDLE

Making a baiting needle for trolling live baits with double loop bridle.

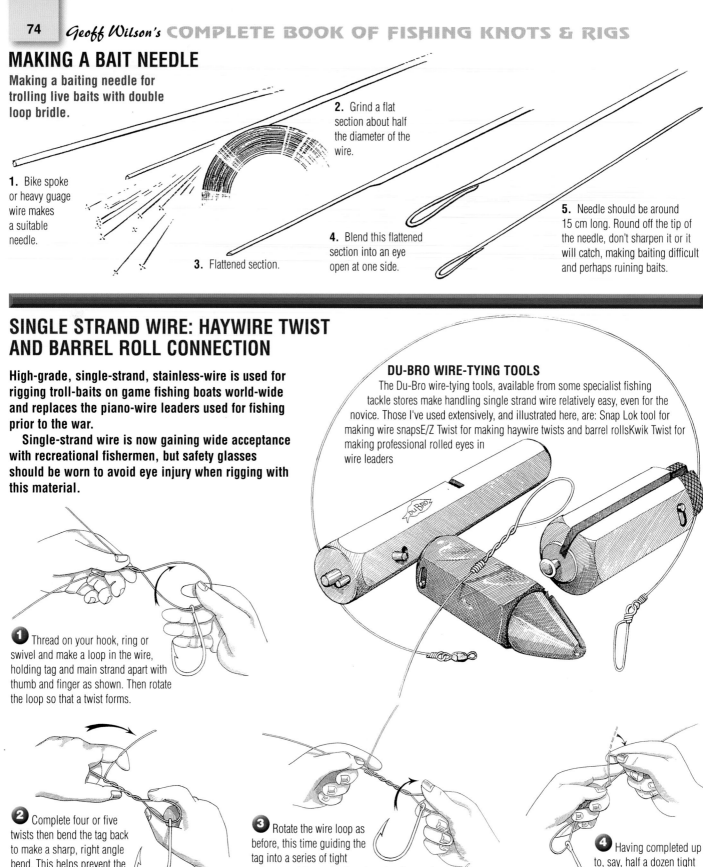

2. Grind a flat section about half the diameter of the wire.

1. Bike spoke or heavy guage wire makes a suitable needle.

3. Flattened section.

4. Blend this flattened section into an eye open at one side.

5. Needle should be around 15 cm long. Round off the tip of the needle, don't sharpen it or it will catch, making baiting difficult and perhaps ruining baits.

SINGLE STRAND WIRE: HAYWIRE TWIST AND BARREL ROLL CONNECTION

High-grade, single-strand, stainless-wire is used for rigging troll-baits on game fishing boats world-wide and replaces the piano-wire leaders used for fishing prior to the war.

Single-strand wire is now gaining wide acceptance with recreational fishermen, but safety glasses should be worn to avoid eye injury when rigging with this material.

DU-BRO WIRE-TYING TOOLS

The Du-Bro wire-tying tools, available from some specialist fishing tackle stores make handling single strand wire relatively easy, even for the novice. Those I've used extensively, and illustrated here, are: Snap Lok tool for making wire snapsE/Z Twist for making haywire twists and barrel rollsKwik Twist for making professional rolled eyes in wire leaders

1 Thread on your hook, ring or swivel and make a loop in the wire, holding tag and main strand apart with thumb and finger as shown. Then rotate the loop so that a twist forms.

2 Complete four or five twists then bend the tag back to make a sharp, right angle bend. This helps prevent the twists springing apart and enables you to begin the next step more easily.

3 Rotate the wire loop as before, this time guiding the tag into a series of tight rolls around the main strand or standing part.

4 Having completed up to, say, half a dozen tight rolls, make a right-angle bend in the tag to form a crank-handle.

5 Holding the barrel-roll firmly between thumb and finger, rotate the crank-handle until the tag snaps off flush with the barrel-rolls.

6 Your connection should look something like this.

RECOMMENDED HOOK

Mustad
10829NPBLN
Big Gun

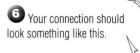

RIGGING WITH WIRE: HEAT WELD WIRE

Wire is used as leader material when seeking sharks, mackerel and other fish with sharp teeth, or which could otherwise sever monofilament leaders. Let's look at making up some rigs using various types of wire, starting with Heat Weld wire.

Heat Weld wire is plastic-coated wire with seven strands. The coating is black and this wire is available under several brands and in a variety of sizes. It is not to be confused with nylon coated wire that cannot be secured with heat.

Attachments in Heat Weld wire may be secured with a crimped sleeve like other multi-strand wire, but for general fishing, as distinct from sport and game fishing, the tag and standing part may be twisted together and sealed with a flame.

3 You may also tie Heat Weld wire to your line using the improved Albright Knot. However, you may have to reduce the number of wraps from ten to eight or the knot could bind before closing.

You have now added a wire trace or leader to your line. This may be all you require. However, should you wish to add a sinker to your rig, take the following steps.

5 We use the Long-liners knot to attach the monofilament dropper to the Lock Weld wire. This is how it is done. Make a loop in the wire and wind the sinker dropper around one side of the loop.

8 Encircle the dropper twice and pass the tag over the two loops then back through the middle.

8a Partially close the knot with gentle pressure on the tag.

1 Thread on your hook ring or swivel and twist the tag and standing part together with a series of haywire twists. Then bend the tag back at right angles to prevent them coming undone.

2 Sear the twists with a match or cigarette lighter to fuse the plastic coating. Don't apply too much heat though or you may remove the plastic coating and defeat the exercise. The tag may be trimmed flush or left around 10 mm in length to secure strip baits as shown in the previous sequence on bait rigging.

4 A sinker may be added using a monofilament dropper. Please yourself whether you tie the dropper to the sinker first as shown here, or you tie the sinker on later.

6 We make three wraps up, winding clockwise, then three wraps back, winding anti-clockwise so the tag and standing part emerge at opposite sides of the wire at the apex of the loop.

7 Close the interlocking loops up a little, but not too much, then encircle the standing part of the dropper with the dropper tag.

9 Grasp the wire loop in one hand, the sinker dropper in the other and pull gently, but firmly, until the knot you just tied slides down onto the loop, and the loop closes. Should the knot bind, or refuse to slide, then you will have to reduce the number of wraps on the wire. Begin reducing by one wrap on the tag side of the loop first.

10 Straighten out the loop in the wire until the dropper locks down hard and will not slide in either direction.

11 This representation clearly shows how the Long-liners Knot "kicks" out the "hook-length" so it doesn't tangle with the dropper when fishing.

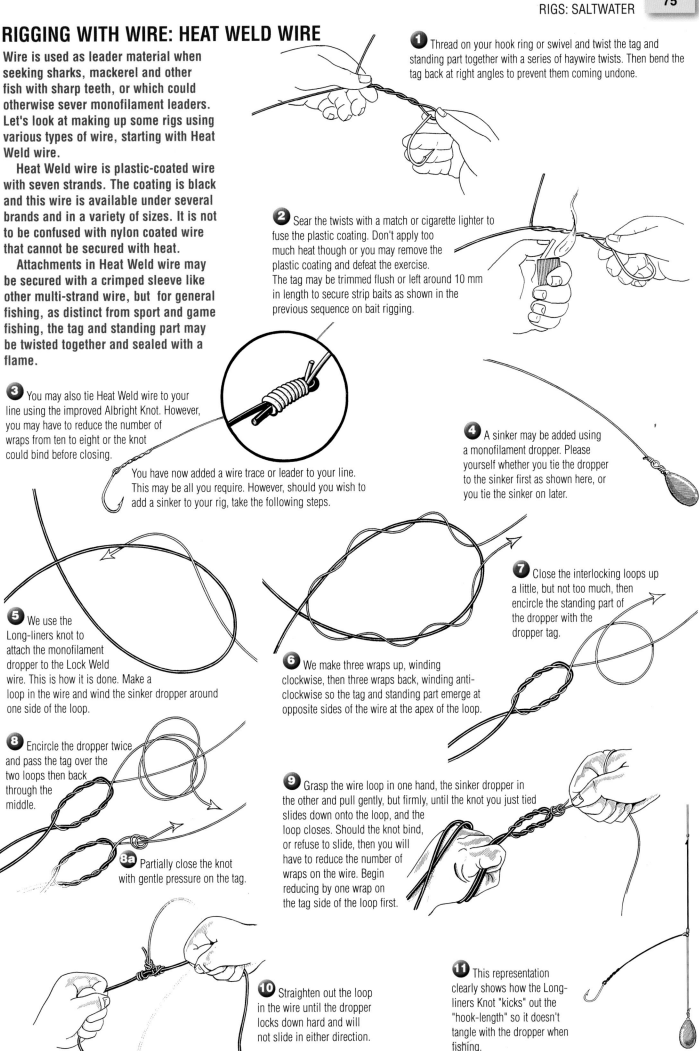

RIGS
FRESHWATER

RIGGING WITH AN EGG-SHAPED BUBBLE FLOAT

Bubble floats are used in freshwater fishing. They are made from clear plastic and may be spherical or egg-shaped.

Bubble floats are designed to be partially filled with water to give them added weight for casting. This is achieved by removing bungs in the spherical float and by displacing the central tube in the egg-shaped float.

The bubble float is rigged as a running float but differs from most running floats in that it does not suspend the baited hook. The baited hook is suspended from a tiny secondary float which is fixed on the line to regulate the depth at which the bait will be presented, and as a stopper on which the bubble rests when being cast out or retrieved.

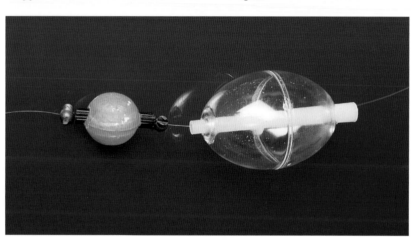

1 Displace the central tube and partially fill the float with water so it will be heavy enough to cast out.

2a Replace the tube and thread your line through the float.

2b Occasionally a small ball sinker is first threaded onto the line. This is only done when the angler is fishing from a windward shore. When the rig is cast out, the sinker rests on the bottom and prevents the rig from being blown ashore.

3 Shown is a length of pliable, extruded foam from which we have cut a short piece for a stopper.

RECOMMENDED HOOK
Mustad
92247
Baitholder

4 Make a hole right through the piece of foam with a needle. Should you use a piece of cork, you will need to heat the needle first so you can burn a hole through it.

5a Thread enough line through your piece of foam for your hook-length or leader.

5b Thread the line back through the foam to fix it into position.

5c I suggest threading the line through the foam a second time, just to make sure it won't slip when you cast out.

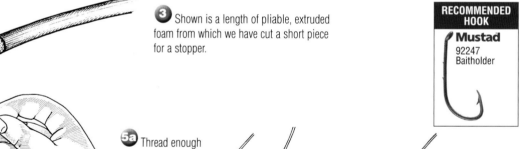

RECOMMENDED HOOK
Mustad
540 French (Viking) Bronzed

6 Shown is the completed rig baited with a dragon fly larva. The baited hook is suspended from the tiny piece of foam so that the fish can take the bait without having to move the bubble float which would probably scare it off.

GENERAL RIGS

A variety of rigs are shown here suitable for fish in rivers and lakes.

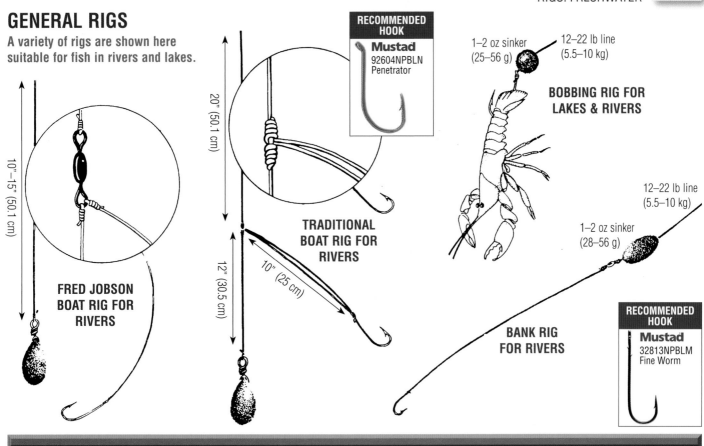

RECOMMENDED HOOK
Mustad
92604NPBLN
Penetrator

20" (50.1 cm)

12" (30.5 cm)

10" (25 cm)

10"–15" (50.1 cm)

FRED JOBSON BOAT RIG FOR RIVERS

TRADITIONAL BOAT RIG FOR RIVERS

1–2 oz sinker (25–56 g)   12–22 lb line (5.5–10 kg)

BOBBING RIG FOR LAKES & RIVERS

12–22 lb line (5.5–10 kg)

1–2 oz sinker (28–56 g)

BANK RIG FOR RIVERS

RECOMMENDED HOOK
Mustad
32813NPBLM
Fine Worm

FRED JOBSON'S TROLLED MUDEYE RIG (DRAGONFLY NYMPH)

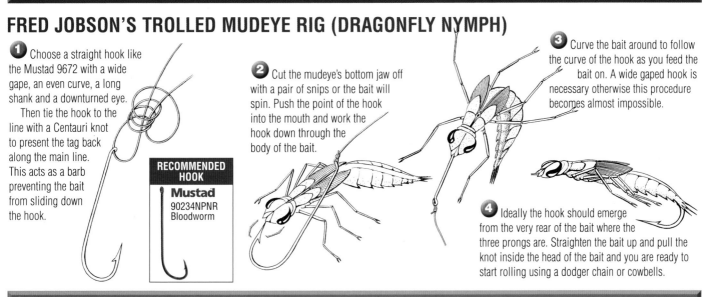

1 Choose a straight hook like the Mustad 9672 with a wide gape, an even curve, a long shank and a downturned eye.
Then tie the hook to the line with a Centauri knot to present the tag back along the main line. This acts as a barb preventing the bait from sliding down the hook.

RECOMMENDED HOOK
Mustad
90234NPNR
Bloodworm

2 Cut the mudeye's bottom jaw off with a pair of snips or the bait will spin. Push the point of the hook into the mouth and work the hook down through the body of the bait.

3 Curve the bait around to follow the curve of the hook as you feed the bait on. A wide gaped hook is necessary otherwise this procedure becomes almost impossible.

4 Ideally the hook should emerge from the very rear of the bait where the three prongs are. Straighten the bait up and pull the knot inside the head of the bait and you are ready to start rolling using a dodger chain or cowbells.

TROLLED SCRUBWORM OR NIGHT CRAWLER

A complicated way to rig a big scrub worm but this is an extremely effective method.

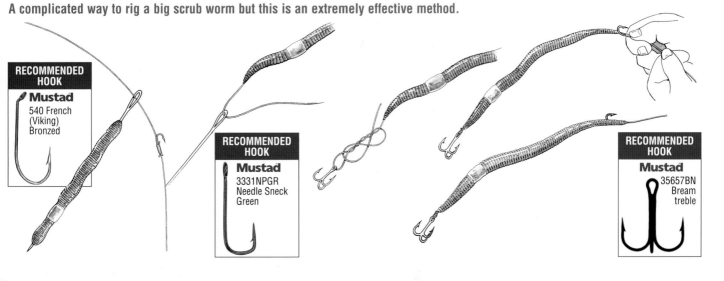

RECOMMENDED HOOK
Mustad
540 French (Viking) Bronzed

RECOMMENDED HOOK
Mustad
3331NPGR
Needle Sneck Green

RECOMMENDED HOOK
Mustad
35657BN
Bream treble

COARSE ANGLING: FLOAT RIGS

Coarse angling techniques are becoming popular. These are the four basic float systems used in coarse angling.

BODIED WAGGLERS

Bodied wagglers are used when straight wagglers patterns prove too light. The most popular bodied wagglers are the peacock stem with a streamlined balsa body, and the more squat bodied onion which has a slightly thinner stem than usually made of light cane.

When to Use

Big bodied wagglers are handy for casting long distances either with or against the wind. The extra body at the base allows more weight to be carried there and hence a potential for longer casts. (N.B. 12-13 ft European graphite float rods are a must for long tangle free casts).Remember at least two thirds of the float's weight carrying capacity needs to go around the base of the the float.

Peacock Stemmed Bodied Waggler

Rigging
Weight so only the tip protrudes.

STRAIGHT WAGGLERS

A quick change float adapter is very handy for quick and easy float changes. Just pull out one float and insert another.

RECOMMENDED HOOK
Mustad
540 French (Viking) Bronzed

There are basically two main types of straight waggler floats —the peacock and the clear plastic.

The straight design of wagglers gives them good buoyancy and excellent visibility at their tip. The time to use these floats is when others become difficult to see either because of the surface chop or when other fine floats are dragging (due to surface drift or river flow). You will find that you can anchor a bait completely with straight wagglers. Remember there is a limit, and once thedrift takes over then alternative methods must be examined.

Shotting guide

Straight wagglers are fixed to the line with two locking shot. Extra shot is best added down the line for stability. Extra shot can be dragged on the bottom to 'slow' or 'still' the bait.

Plastics

The clear plastics are designed for shallow water. They won't spook fish by throwing a heavy shadow. These floats work so well that most use them now regardless of depth!

PLASTIC STEM STICKS

Manufacturers have switched now to plastic in nearly all stick floats.

Plastic certainly offers a different dimension in tackle presentation. Sticks with synthetic stems work best in shallow to medium depths and up to moderate flows of water. A recent innovation has been to make the base out of clear plastic to help eliminate shadows.

The top third of the body in all cases is made from balsa.

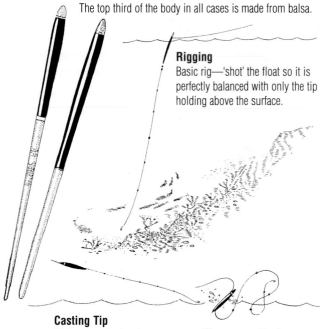

Rigging
Basic rig—'shot' the float so it is perfectly balanced with only the tip holding above the surface.

Casting Tip
Right way—feather the line out just before it touches down.

Wrong way—Don't dump the rig on the water.

SLIDER FLOATS

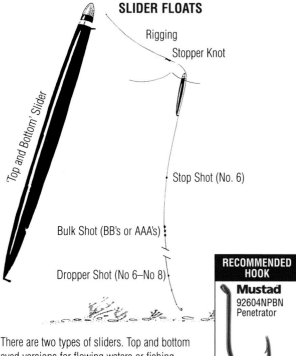

'Top and Bottom' Slider

Rigging
Stopper Knot

Stop Shot (No. 6)

Bulk Shot (BB's or AAA's)

Dropper Shot (No 6–No 8)

RECOMMENDED HOOK
Mustad
92604NPBN Penetrator

There are two types of sliders. Top and bottom eyed versions for flowing waters or fishing close range and bottom enders for long distance casting.

The top and bottom sliders are made completely from balsa and have the capacity to carry between two and six AAA shot. The bottom end has a balsa or plastic body and a peacock stem. Sliders are used with a float rig to set the bait deeper than the length of your rod. Sliders are rigged as running floats and can be effective to depths of 30 feet (10 metres) or more!

They can of course be used in shallow water, a good example would be when backside foliage makes casting stick floats impossible. Here a slider may be cast considerable distance underarm.

COARSE ANGLING: SWIMFEEDER RIGS

Feeders act as a sinker as well as a carrier and dispenser of berley. These rigs are extremely effective on bottom dwelling species in fresh water and also salt water.

SHOCK BEADS
When using swivels or stopping knots as on the loop rig, you may find that the feeder may cause damage to knots. By using soft ledger beads we are effectively using a shock absorber between our knot and feeder, eliminating knot fatigue.

Loop Rig
The Loop Rig has the same advantages as the stop shot rig, however, the extra loop or loops at the base of the rig act as an anti-tangle device eliminating the use of a feeder boom. This rig is popular when fishing long range tactics on stillwaters, but it will not prevent tangles in very fast currents.

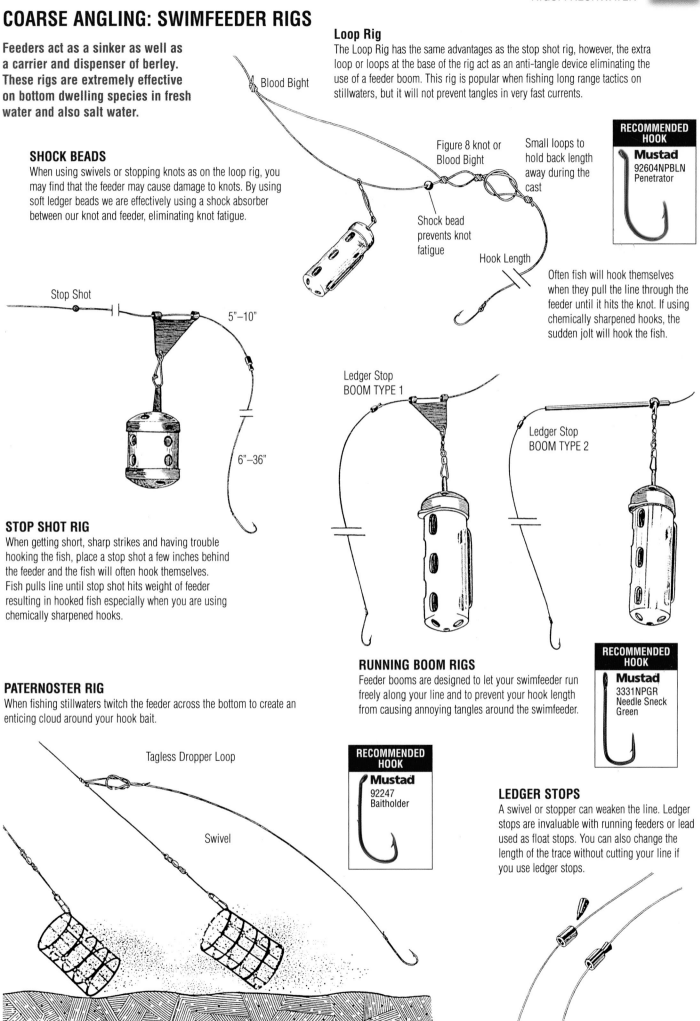

Blood Bight

Figure 8 knot or Blood Bight

Small loops to hold back length away during the cast

Shock bead prevents knot fatigue

Hook Length

RECOMMENDED HOOK
Mustad
92604NPBLN
Penetrator

Often fish will hook themselves when they pull the line through the feeder until it hits the knot. If using chemically sharpened hooks, the sudden jolt will hook the fish.

Stop Shot

5"–10"

6"–36"

STOP SHOT RIG
When getting short, sharp strikes and having trouble hooking the fish, place a stop shot a few inches behind the feeder and the fish will often hook themselves. Fish pulls line until stop shot hits weight of feeder resulting in hooked fish especially when you are using chemically sharpened hooks.

Ledger Stop BOOM TYPE 1

Ledger Stop BOOM TYPE 2

PATERNOSTER RIG
When fishing stillwaters twitch the feeder across the bottom to create an enticing cloud around your hook bait.

Tagless Dropper Loop

Swivel

RUNNING BOOM RIGS
Feeder booms are designed to let your swimfeeder run freely along your line and to prevent your hook length from causing annoying tangles around the swimfeeder.

RECOMMENDED HOOK
Mustad
3331NPGR
Needle Sneck
Green

RECOMMENDED HOOK
Mustad
92247
Baitholder

LEDGER STOPS
A swivel or stopper can weaken the line. Ledger stops are invaluable with running feeders or lead used as float stops. You can also change the length of the trace without cutting your line if you use ledger stops.

BUMPER KNOT OR SALMON EGG LOOP

This knot produces a loop along the shank of the hook enabling the use of soft, delicate baits like salmon roe. When tested this knot retained the full breaking strain of the line.

RECOMMENDED HOOK

Mustad
92553NPBN
Beak Bait
Hooks

1 Begin with 24 to 30 inches (60 to 80 cm) of leader material and thread one end through the eye of the hook.

2 Adjust the length of the tag to the length of the hook and begin wrapping the shank of the hook, and tag, with the standing part of the leader. Wrapping in an anti-clockwise direction is suggested because this makes finishing the knot easier.

3 Make a series of tight wraps down the shank of the hook. Eight wraps are shown here but the number of wraps is determined by the size of loop required. Then thread the other end of the leader back through the eye of the hook leaving a loop large enough to make several more wraps around the hook.

4 Turn the hook around the other way and commence wrapping the entire hook and standing part of the leader – the part you just passed back through the eye of the hook – with the loop.

5 Make another six or seven wraps.

6 Close the loop by extracting the standing part of the leader with one hand while holding the wraps against the hook with the other.

7 Trim the tag up short and the knot is finished.

DOUBLE HOOK BUMPER KNOT

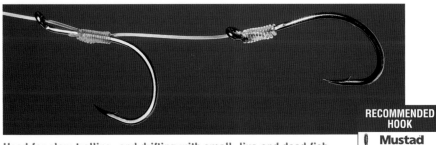

RECOMMENDED HOOK

Mustad
34007
O'Shaughnessy

Used for slow-trolling, and drifting with small, live and dead fish baits for a variety of salt and freshwater predators, the double hook Bumper knot is well worth learning how to tie.

After adding a second hook to the leader, it was shown during testing that premature separations could occur if the eye of the hook was threaded before wrapping was commenced. This happened when weight was exerted on the bottom hook causing the line to pinch down into the gap between the end of the wire forming the eye and the shank of the hook. The problem was completely overcome by using the following strategy.

1 Lay the standing part of the line alongside the second hook to be added and twist a loop into the line near the eye of the hook as shown.

2 Commence a series of tight wraps down the shank of the hook, just as we did when attaching the first hook.

3 Having made eight or nine wraps, thread the standing part of the line back through the eye of the hook leaving a sufficiently large loop to bind around the shank of the hook being added, and the hook already attached.

4 The method of wrapping the added hook is shown and becomes relatively easy with practice.

5 Close the loop as we did with the single hook Bumper knot and trim the tag.

RIGGING SPINNERBAITS

Cameron Jones devised this inventive method to allow quick changing spinnerbaits.

1 Wire snaps are great for attaching spinner baits, no doubt of that.

2 Trouble is, sometimes the snap slides up one of the arms, ruining the presentation.

3 This can be prevented by a short length of plastic tube, the type used for aquarium aerators.

4 Just slide the piece of hose over the bend in the wire before attaching the snap.

5 The problem is solved.

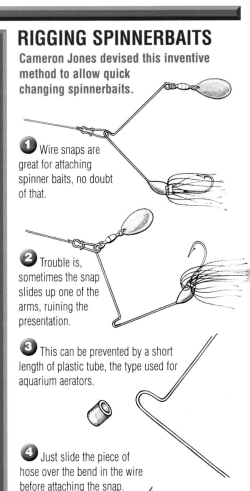

HOW TO HOOK FRESHWATER BAITS

SCRUBWORMS
Earthworms and scrubworms are excellent bait for most freshwater species. They may be used singly or in a bunch of two or more as shown in these diagrams.

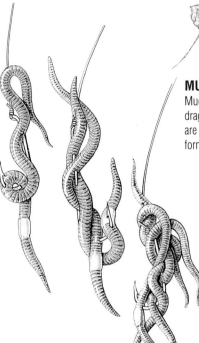

CATERPILLAR
Best hooked through the body.

MUDEYES
Mudeyes, the aquatic larval form of various dragon flies, are prized for bait. Mostly they are used live, the hook penetrating their newly forming wings.

RECOMMENDED HOOK
Mustad
3331NPGR
Needle Sneck
Green

GRASSHOPPERS
Grasshoppers are most effective when lightly hooked and drifted downstream while the angler feeds out slack line.

MAGGOTS
Blowfly maggots are used in fresh water for a wide variety of fish, but will take saltwater species like garfish, bream and whiting to name just a few. Maggots are hooked in the tail (large) end on a small hook say size 12 down to 16. They may be used singly or several at a time.

BARDI GRUBS
Bardi grubs are a great Murray cod bait. They are best fished alive but will soon die and discolour if pierced with the hook. This is why we bind bardi grubs to the hook with the elastic thread Bait Mate to which we referred earlier.

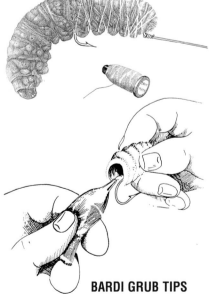

BARDI GRUB TIPS
To best prepare bardi grubs for storage, blanche grubs in boiling water for 28 seconds and freeze overnight. Then store in freezer bags—almost as good as fresh baits and will keep for ages.

Try Fred Jobson's method to make bardi grubs irresistible by cutting a large fresh grub in half and filling the body of the grub with a fish scent, such as Halco Scent.

FRESHWATER CRAYFISH
Freshwater crayfish are usually fished live with the hook through the tail, with or without a running sinker. Remove or break the moveable joint on pincers to prevent it from crawling under snags.

When using dead crayfish crush the body to bet out all juices. Place a piece of bardi grub on hook end as shown.

SHRIMPS
Hook in tail and always use live if possible. They can be single hooked backwards or double rigged with the hook through both tails.

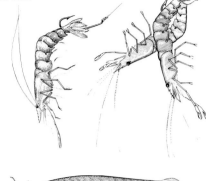

MINNOWS & GALAXIDS
Minnow are used for trout in fresh water. Two minnow hooked on the same hook will often be taken eagerly when single presentations are ignored. Try any of the presentations shown, twin minnow hooked through tail, above the lateral line behind the shoulder, through the upper jaw or with two hooks and a half hitch on the tail.

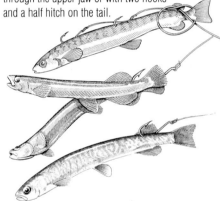

WHITEBAIT & GLASSIES
Hook through gill and eye with a half hitch on the tail. Also can employ a free running hook and attach just forward of tail. To rig whitebait for trolling behind a downrigger hook through the jaw and again under the belly.

RECOMMENDED HOOK
Mustad
92604NPBLN
Penetrator

RIGGING WITH LEAD-CORED LINE FOR TROLLING

Lead-Cored line is used by anglers who want to troll their bait or lure substantially below the surface without additional paraphernalia like down-rigging weights or paravanes.

Lead-Cored line consists of a continuous strand of lead wire inside a hollow, braided, dacron line. The dacron is coloured coded with a colour change every ten yards (9 metres) so the angler knows how much line is out.

Lead-Cored dacron lines come in various sizes from 12 pounds (5.5 kg) to 45 pounds (21 kg) breaking strain. The lead wire remains the same for all line sizes so the lighter gauge Lead-Cored lines will run deeper than the heavier ones, that's provided that the trolling speed, leader and lure size remain the same.

Lead-Cored lines work best when loop-spliced at both ends. One end being attached to the backing, or fishing line already on the reel, the other end being attached to a monofilament leader several metres long which can also be wound onto the reel. The lure or baited hook is attached to this leader.

MATERIALS:
Needle: A fine gauge Top Shot loop-splicing needle—or a length of .014" (0.356 mm)—stainless wire bent double to form a needle. **Glue:** Super Glue or Top Shot Supertac.

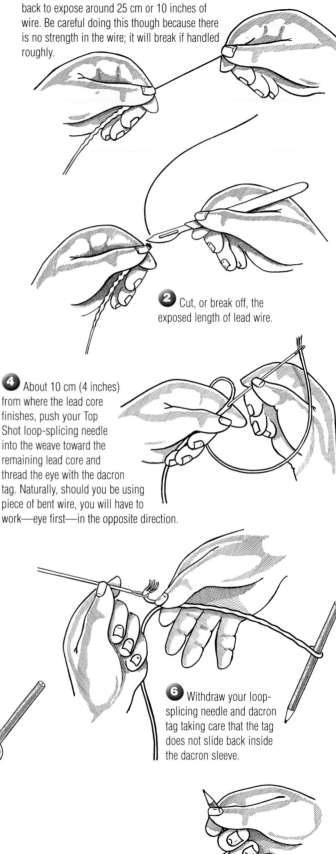

1 Expose the lead core and push the dacron back to expose around 25 cm or 10 inches of wire. Be careful doing this though because there is no strength in the wire; it will break if handled roughly.

2 Cut, or break off, the exposed length of lead wire.

3 Extend the dacron sleeve to its former position. This will leave you with 25 cm or so of hollow dacron to make your first loop splice.

4 About 10 cm (4 inches) from where the lead core finishes, push your Top Shot loop-splicing needle into the weave toward the remaining lead core and thread the eye with the dacron tag. Naturally, should you be using piece of bent wire, you will have to work—eye first—in the opposite direction.

5 Work your Top Shot loop-splicing needle all the way up to where the lead wire ends, but put a loop gauge, or pencil as I have done, into the loop so that it won't close completely.

6 Withdraw your loop-splicing needle and dacron tag taking care that the tag does not slide back inside the dacron sleeve.

8 Smear the tag with glue, bearing in mind the nature of the glue you are using: Superglue and Supertac require minimal application. Slow curing glues more liberal application.

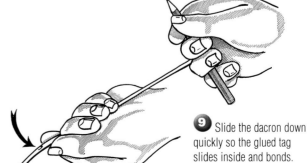

9 Slide the dacron down quickly so the glued tag slides inside and bonds.

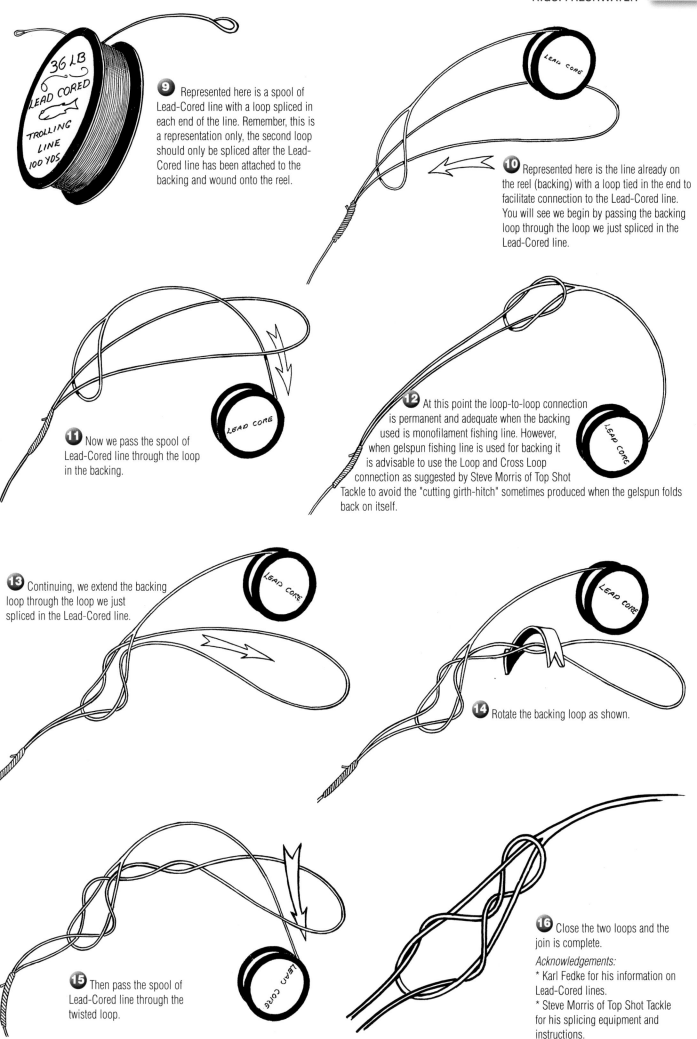

36 LB LEAD CORED TROLLING LINE 100 YDS

9 Represented here is a spool of Lead-Cored line with a loop spliced in each end of the line. Remember, this is a representation only, the second loop should only be spliced after the Lead-Cored line has been attached to the backing and wound onto the reel.

10 Represented here is the line already on the reel (backing) with a loop tied in the end to facilitate connection to the Lead-Cored line. You will see we begin by passing the backing loop through the loop we just spliced in the Lead-Cored line.

11 Now we pass the spool of Lead-Cored line through the loop in the backing.

12 At this point the loop-to-loop connection is permanent and adequate when the backing used is monofilament fishing line. However, when gelspun fishing line is used for backing it is advisable to use the Loop and Cross Loop connection as suggested by Steve Morris of Top Shot Tackle to avoid the "cutting girth-hitch" sometimes produced when the gelspun folds back on itself.

13 Continuing, we extend the backing loop through the loop we just spliced in the Lead-Cored line.

14 Rotate the backing loop as shown.

15 Then pass the spool of Lead-Cored line through the twisted loop.

16 Close the two loops and the join is complete.

Acknowledgements:
* Karl Fedke for his information on Lead-Cored lines.
* Steve Morris of Top Shot Tackle for his splicing equipment and instructions.

SOFT PLASTIC RIGS

TEXAS RIG

The advantage of Texas rigging a worm is to allow the angler to fish in heavy cover without hanging up. Use an intermittent and slow retrieve.

CAROLINA RIG

This is a very effective rig for covering lots of water fast. Best used off points and on humps. Slow retrieve.

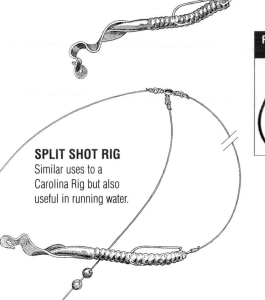

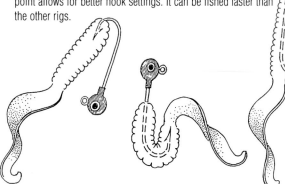

RECOMMENDED HOOK

Mustad
38101BLN
Grip Pin
Ultra Point
Hook

SPLIT SHOT RIG

Similar uses to a Carolina Rig but also useful in running water.

RIGGING A JIG HEAD

Jigs are an effective presentation for soft plastics. The exposed point allows for better hook settings. It can be fished faster than the other rigs.

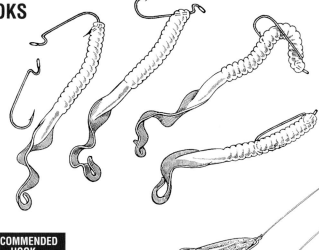

RIGGING RUBBER WORMS ON WORM HOOKS

HOW TO RIG A RUBBER WORM HOOK: BERKLEY

To rig a worm, start the hook in the nose of the bait and bring it out 1/4 inch from the nose. Slide the worm up over the eye and rotate the hook 180º and re-enter and push the hook back until it's just under the surface of the worm.

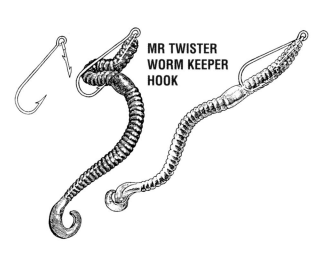

MR TWISTER WORM KEEPER HOOK

RECOMMENDED HOOK

Mustad
38101BLN
Grip Pin
Ultra Point
Hook

RENOSKI EASY WORM HOOK

MUSTAD POWER LOCK WORM HOOK

MUSTAD WEIGHTED WORM HOOK WITH POWER LOCK

MUSTAD WEIGHTED WORM HOOK

DOWNRIGGING

Downrigging has grown in popularity in fresh water and is now recognised as being an important technique in taking salmonids from deep lakes.
  Stacking, sliding and dual rod rigs are all shown here.

When using two rods on one downrigger they must sit in rod holders angled away from each other.

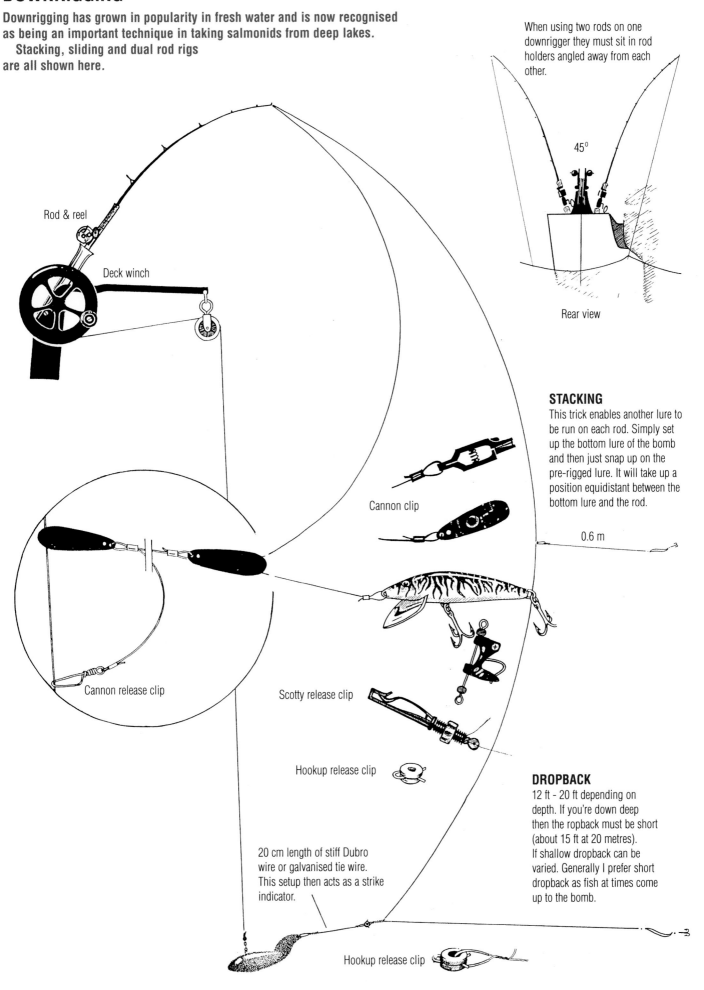

45°

Rear view

Rod & reel

Deck winch

Cannon clip

Cannon release clip

Scotty release clip

Hookup release clip

20 cm length of stiff Dubro wire or galvanised tie wire. This setup then acts as a strike indicator.

Hookup release clip

STACKING

This trick enables another lure to be run on each rod. Simply set up the bottom lure of the bomb and then just snap up on the pre-rigged lure. It will take up a position equidistant between the bottom lure and the rod.

0.6 m

DROPBACK

12 ft - 20 ft depending on depth. If you're down deep then the ropback must be short (about 15 ft at 20 metres). If shallow dropback can be varied. Generally I prefer short dropback as fish at times come up to the bomb.

RIGS
GAME & SPORT

RIGGING A STRIP BAIT

This is an excellent way of rigging an unweighted strip bait on heavy tackle. It is ideally suited for drifting down a berley trail because it can be deployed and retrieved continually without deforming or spinning.

Your leader may be heavy nylon monofilament or multistrand wire and your hook should be straight, not kirbed or reversed, because this may cause the bait to spin.

In addition to your hook, leader and bait, you will need a length of 0.7 mm galvanised tie wire which is available from almost every hardware store. Should 0.7 mm not be available, you can use 0.8 mm.

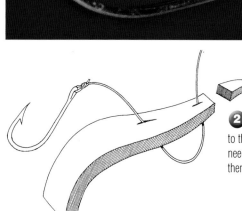

1 First cut a suitable strip, either from a small tuna or other oily fish. The strip should be in the shape of an elongated, isosceles triangle.

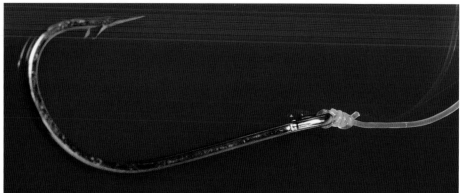

2 Cut off the pointed end so there is some width to the narrowest end. Then, using your hook as a needle, draw your leader through at the narrow end, then back again about a third of the way down.

3 Turn you hook around and, with the point of the hook facing away from the leader and down toward the end of the bait, push it into the skin side of the strip.

4 Then back out the same side so the point of the hook emerges from the bait near the end of the strip. Having secured the hook in the bait, we now need to secure the leader to the bait with the galvanised tie wire. Push a 30 cm or so length through the bait where you first punctured it with the hook.

5 With the bait central on the wire, bend both wire tags back along the leader and, beginning as close as practical to the end of the strip, wind one tag tightly around the other, and the leader, in series of barrel rolls.

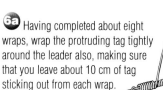

6a Having completed about eight wraps, wrap the protruding tag tightly around the leader also, making sure that you leave about 10 cm of tag sticking out from each wrap.

6b To break the tags off close to the wraps, we bend the tag over so that it forms a handle or crank. Do this with each tag in turn.

6c Using the handle you have made, wind the tag around until it breaks off. Do each in turn so that there are no sharp tags to catch in your hand or clothing.

7 Shown is the completed bait.

RECOMMENDED HOOK

Mustad
92554NPNR
Big Red

RECOMMENDED HOOK

Mustad
34007
O'Shaughnessy

LIVE BAIT ON GANGED HOOKS FOR SPANISH MACKEREL

Although captures on this rig are not acceptable under IGFA rules, this is an ideal rig for catching large mackerel.

RECOMMENDED HOOK

Mustad
4202D
Kirby Ringed –
Duratin
(open eyes)

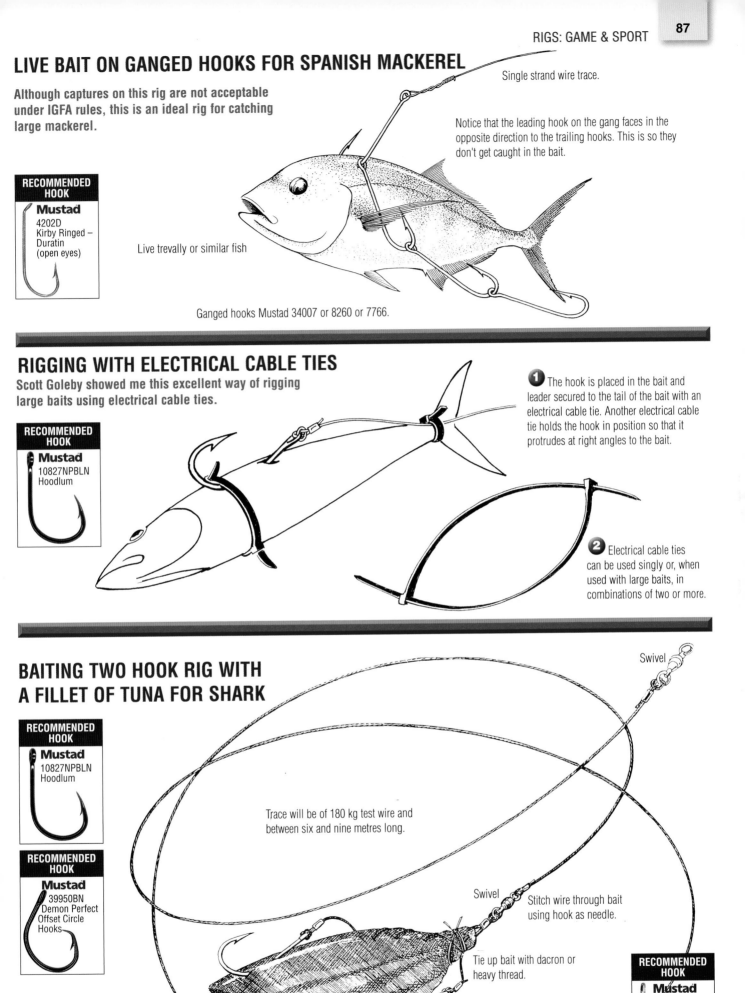

Single strand wire trace.

Notice that the leading hook on the gang faces in the opposite direction to the trailing hooks. This is so they don't get caught in the bait.

Live trevally or similar fish

Ganged hooks Mustad 34007 or 8260 or 7766.

RIGGING WITH ELECTRICAL CABLE TIES

Scott Goleby showed me this excellent way of rigging large baits using electrical cable ties.

RECOMMENDED HOOK

Mustad
10827NPBLN
Hoodlum

1 The hook is placed in the bait and leader secured to the tail of the bait with an electrical cable tie. Another electrical cable tie holds the hook in position so that it protrudes at right angles to the bait.

2 Electrical cable ties can be used singly or, when used with large baits, in combinations of two or more.

BAITING TWO HOOK RIG WITH A FILLET OF TUNA FOR SHARK

RECOMMENDED HOOK

Mustad
10827NPBLN
Hoodlum

RECOMMENDED HOOK

Mustad
39950BN
Demon Perfect
Offset Circle
Hooks

Swivel

Trace will be of 180 kg test wire and between six and nine metres long.

Swivel

Stitch wire through bait using hook as needle.

Tie up bait with dacron or heavy thread.

RECOMMENDED HOOK

Mustad
7766D Tarpon
Ringed

Hooks are placed on the outside of tuna fillet by pushing point in, then out through the skin.

Mustad 7766 size 12/0–14/0

MAKING A DOUBLE LOOP BRIDLE FOR LIVE BAIT TROLLING

Towing bridles for live bait trolling vary a good deal. We use the double-loop bridle pre-tied in monofilament because it allows the bait to be attached and placed back in the water in the shortest possible time: This is around 15 seconds for practised operators. To make a double-loop bridle we need a rigged leader with a suitable hook attached, a length of 24 kg monofilament or thereabouts, an open-eye live-baiting needle (see page 74) and a loop gauge which can be a pencil or pen.

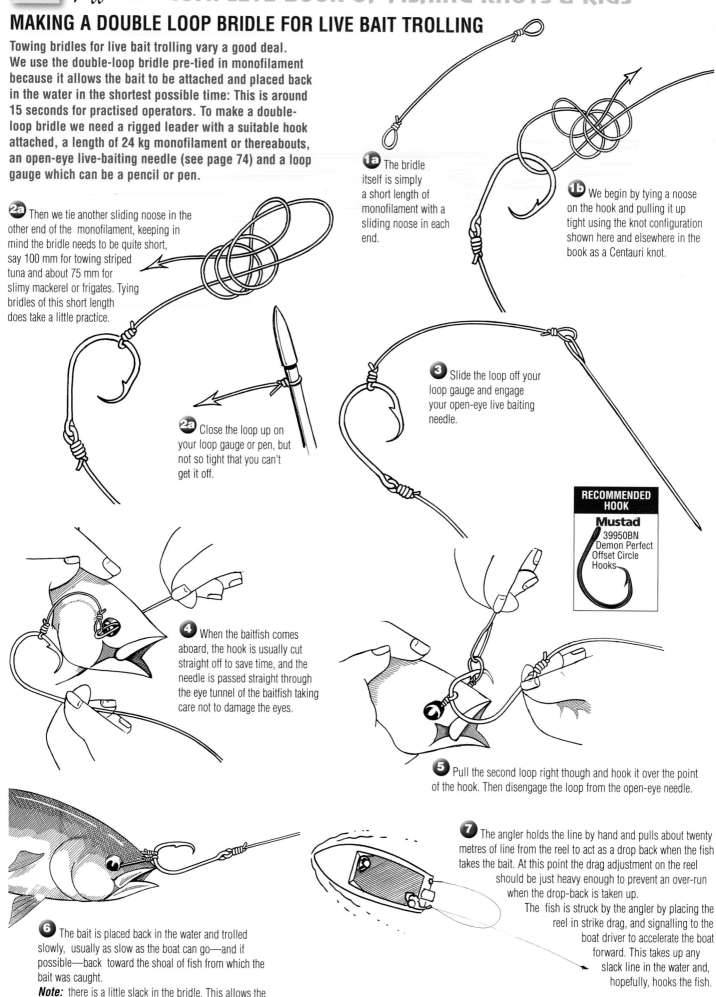

1a The bridle itself is simply a short length of monofilament with a sliding noose in each end.

1b We begin by tying a noose on the hook and pulling it up tight using the knot configuration shown here and elsewhere in the book as a Centauri knot.

2a Then we tie another sliding noose in the other end of the monofilament, keeping in mind the bridle needs to be quite short, say 100 mm for towing striped tuna and about 75 mm for slimy mackerel or frigates. Tying bridles of this short length does take a little practice.

2a Close the loop up on your loop gauge or pen, but not so tight that you can't get it off.

3 Slide the loop off your loop gauge and engage your open-eye live baiting needle.

RECOMMENDED HOOK

Mustad
39950BN
Demon Perfect
Offset Circle
Hooks

4 When the baitfish comes aboard, the hook is usually cut straight off to save time, and the needle is passed straight through the eye tunnel of the baitfish taking care not to damage the eyes.

5 Pull the second loop right though and hook it over the point of the hook. Then disengage the loop from the open-eye needle.

6 The bait is placed back in the water and trolled slowly, usually as slow as the boat can go—and if possible—back toward the shoal of fish from which the bait was caught.
Note: there is a little slack in the bridle. This allows the hook to fold bait easily when it is taken by the game fish. Anglers who rig the hook too tightly on the head miss fish because of this.

7 The angler holds the line by hand and pulls about twenty metres of line from the reel to act as a drop back when the fish takes the bait. At this point the drag adjustment on the reel should be just heavy enough to prevent an over-run when the drop-back is taken up.
The fish is struck by the angler by placing the reel in strike drag, and signalling to the boat driver to accelerate the boat forward. This takes up any slack line in the water and, hopefully, hooks the fish.

RIGGING A GARFISH AS A SKIP BAIT

Garfish may be rigged as skip baits on either heavy monofilament or wire. This method deals with rigging a garfish on monofilament but 49 strand cable could be substituted where mackerel or other "toothy critters" are sought.

To rig this bait you will need a large garfish, a length of heavy monofilament or 49 strand cable with a suitable size hook for the garfish you are using, and a roll of 0.7 or 0.8 mm galvanised tie wire which is available in hardware stores. An awl or stout needle is also useful for making pilot holes for the wire.

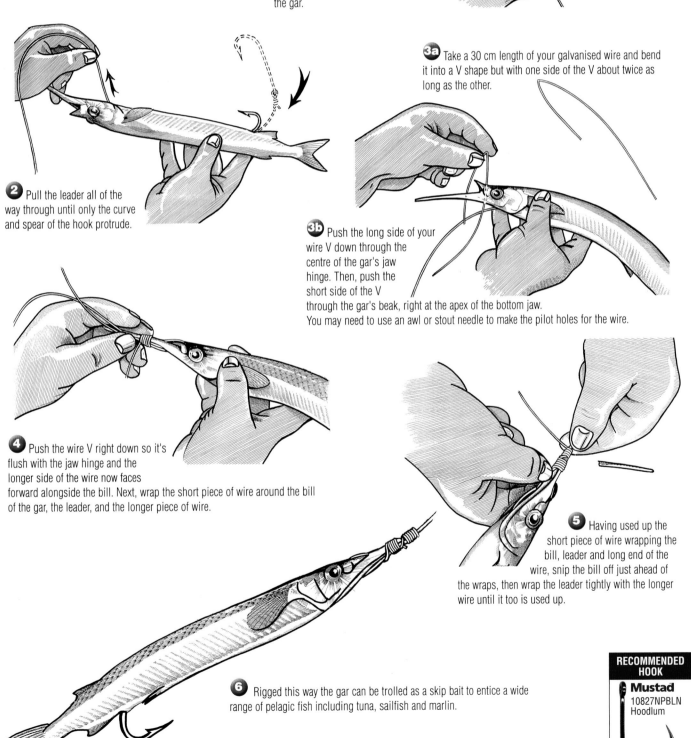

1 Begin by taking 60 cm or so of the galvanised wire, bending it over and twisting it together to form a baiting needle.

Push the rounded end into the gills of the gar, down through body and out of its anus. Then, thread the bend in the wire with your leader and draw it inside the body of the gar.

2 Pull the leader all of the way through until only the curve and spear of the hook protrude.

3a Take a 30 cm length of your galvanised wire and bend it into a V shape but with one side of the V about twice as long as the other.

3b Push the long side of your wire V down through the centre of the gar's jaw hinge. Then, push the short side of the V through the gar's beak, right at the apex of the bottom jaw. You may need to use an awl or stout needle to make the pilot holes for the wire.

4 Push the wire V right down so it's flush with the jaw hinge and the longer side of the wire now faces forward alongside the bill. Next, wrap the short piece of wire around the bill of the gar, the leader, and the longer piece of wire.

5 Having used up the short piece of wire wrapping the bill, leader and long end of the wire, snip the bill off just ahead of the wraps, then wrap the leader tightly with the longer wire until it too is used up.

6 Rigged this way the gar can be trolled as a skip bait to entice a wide range of pelagic fish including tuna, sailfish and marlin.

RECOMMENDED HOOK

Mustad
10827NPBLN
Hoodlum

RIGGING A GARFISH (BALAO) AS A SWIMMING BAIT

This bait is shown rigged with a "stinger", a short length of flexible wire to present the hook in the rear of the bait to maximise hook-ups on all species of game fish.

The stingers are made up separately in various lengths to suit different size baits and kept on hand for rigging as the opportunity arises.

To rig this bait you will need suitable fish like a gar, pike or longtom, a stinger rigged with a short length of forty nine strand wire, a length of .08 mm galvanised wire for making a baiting needle, a large barrel sinker or, for larger baits a large bean or leadline sinker, a length of heavy dacron and and an awl form making a pilot hole for the wire leader. You will also need a roll of single strand wire like the .029 inch stainless steel used in my model.

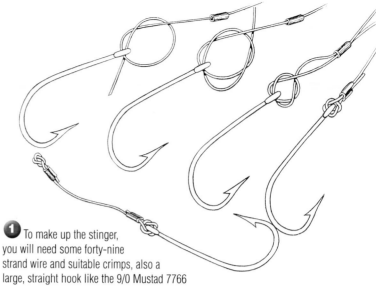

1 To make up the stinger, you will need some forty-nine strand wire and suitable crimps, also a large, straight hook like the 9/0 Mustad 7766 used in the model. The hook is secured with a Flemish Eye and crimp. The stages of forming the eye are shown. A Flemish Eye is also formed in the other end of the wire.

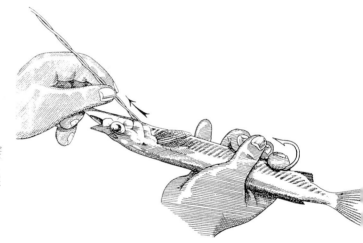

2 Take a 60 cm length of galvanised wire, bend it over and twist it together to form a baiting needle. In this application, we bend the U into a small hook. Pass the baiting needle into the gills of the bait, down through the body and out of the bait's anus. Hook the eye of the stingerand draw it back into the body of the bait.

3 Having pulled the stinger inside the bait, hold the protruding hook and body of the gar in one hand while exerting pressure on the baiting needle with the other so the little hook we made straightens out and the wire needle comes away leaving the stinger in place.

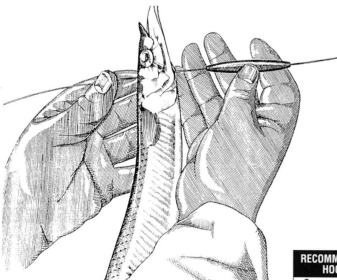

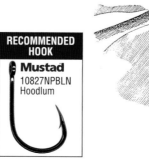

RECOMMENDED HOOK

Mustad
10827NPBLN
Hoodlum

4 Make a pilot's hole in the top of the bait's head, a short distance behind the eye. Pass the leader down through the hole so that it engages the eye of the stinger and emerges under the bait's head. This is the trickiest part of the whole operation. Complete this step by threading on the sinker.

5 Bend the wire forward so that the sinker fits snugly under the bait's bottom jaw. If it doesn't fit, then you are using the wrong size sinker.

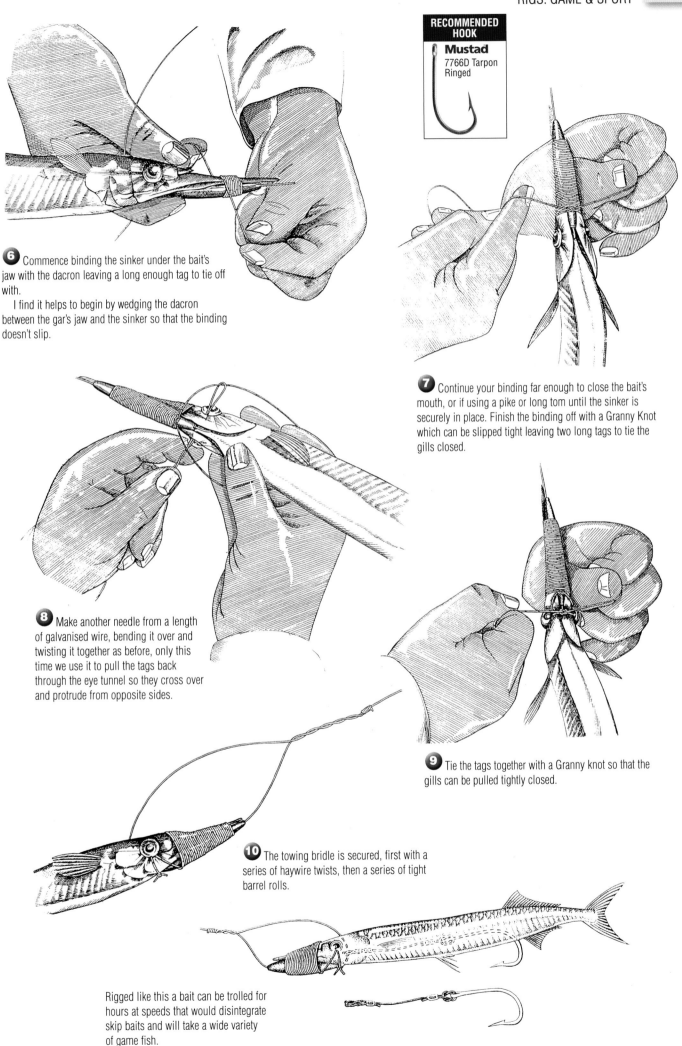

RECOMMENDED HOOK

Mustad
7766D Tarpon
Ringed

6 Commence binding the sinker under the bait's jaw with the dacron leaving a long enough tag to tie off with.

I find it helps to begin by wedging the dacron between the gar's jaw and the sinker so that the binding doesn't slip.

7 Continue your binding far enough to close the bait's mouth, or if using a pike or long tom until the sinker is securely in place. Finish the binding off with a Granny Knot which can be slipped tight leaving two long tags to tie the gills closed.

8 Make another needle from a length of galvanised wire, bending it over and twisting it together as before, only this time we use it to pull the tags back through the eye tunnel so they cross over and protrude from opposite sides.

9 Tie the tags together with a Granny knot so that the gills can be pulled tightly closed.

10 The towing bridle is secured, first with a series of haywire twists, then a series of tight barrel rolls.

Rigged like this a bait can be trolled for hours at speeds that would disintegrate skip baits and will take a wide variety of game fish.

HOW TO RIG A SQUID FOR TROLLING OR DRIFTING

All game fish feed on squid, in fact they probably eat more squid than anything else. Yet most game fishermen, partly through convenience and partly through ignorance of this fact, are content to use lures.

The lures game fishermen use resemble squid; the skirt resembles the tentacles trailing behind the body, while some lure makers even attach large eyes to their lures to resemble the large eyes of the squid.

While skirted game fishing lures are usually well made and attractive to both fish and the anglers who fish for them, nothing is as effective as the real thing—not even close. Freshly caught squid, or squid which have been quickly frozen shortly after capture, will out-fish lures by a wide margin if rigged correctly. Let's look at how it is done. To rig a squid for trolling or drifting you will need a length of leader material; either heavy monofilament of multi-strand wire, a suitable hook like the Mustad 7731 or Sea Demon, in size 8/0 to 10/0, and about one metre of 0.8 mm galvanised tie-wire, an item which you can buy in almost any hardware store. You will also require a sharp knife or pair of scissors.

1a Break your metre length of wire in two halves. Fold one length over to form a double strand and twist it together to make a rigid baiting needle with an eye.

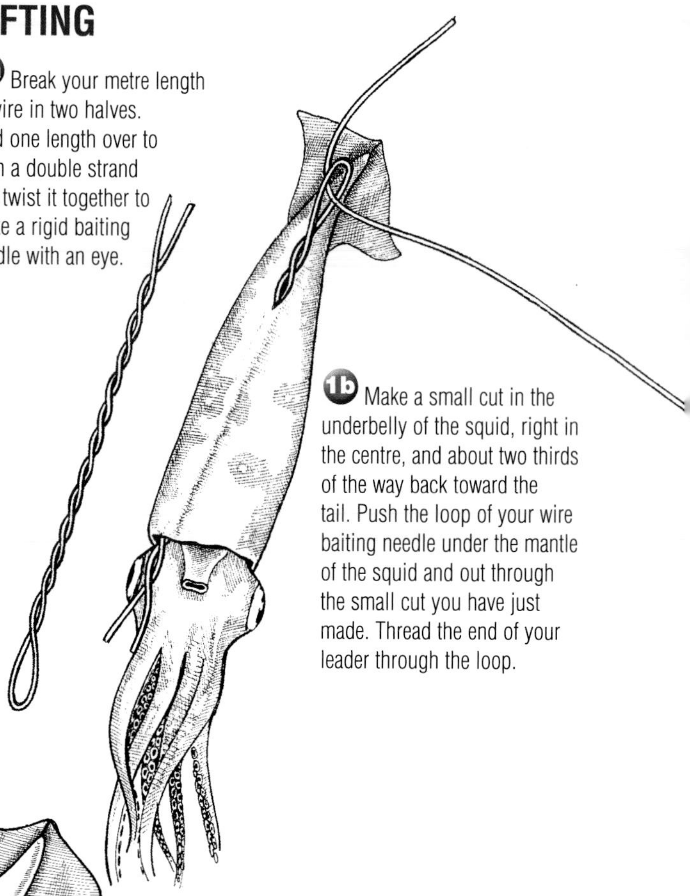

1b Make a small cut in the underbelly of the squid, right in the centre, and about two thirds of the way back toward the tail. Push the loop of your wire baiting needle under the mantle of the squid and out through the small cut you have just made. Thread the end of your leader through the loop.

2a Retrieve your baiting needle from the squid's mantle, pulling the end of the leader through with it.

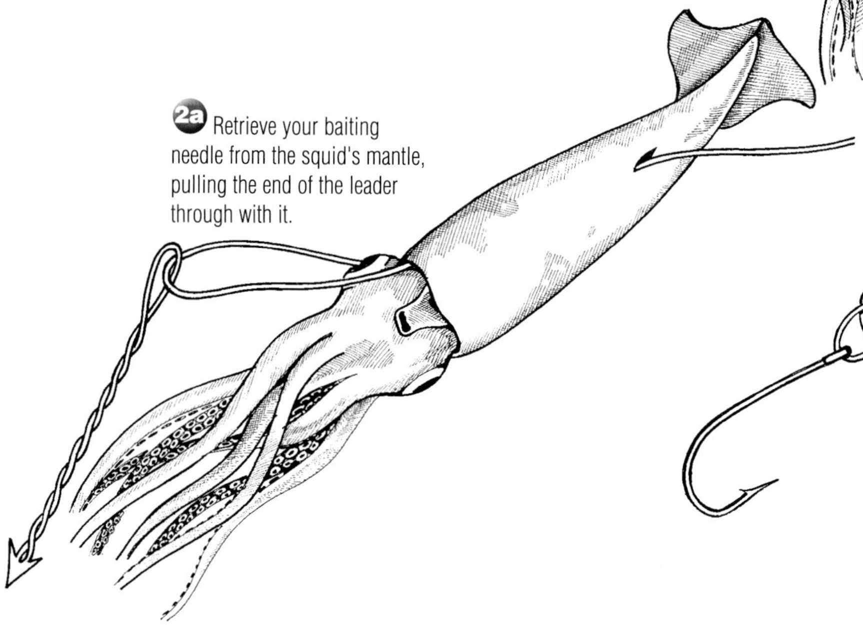

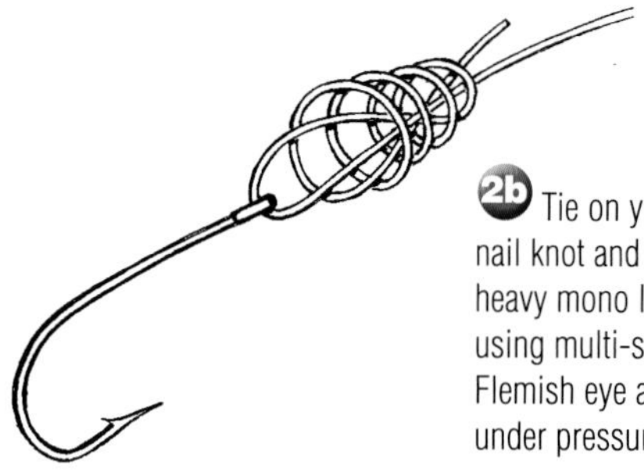

2b Tie on your hook. Shown here is the nail knot and loop most suitable for very heavy mono leaders. Naturally, should you be using multi-strand wire, you will need to tie a Flemish eye and crimp it so that it won't slip under pressure.

3a Having attached your hook to the leader, you now have to insert it in the bait. Start under the head with the hook point facing back toward the tentacles.

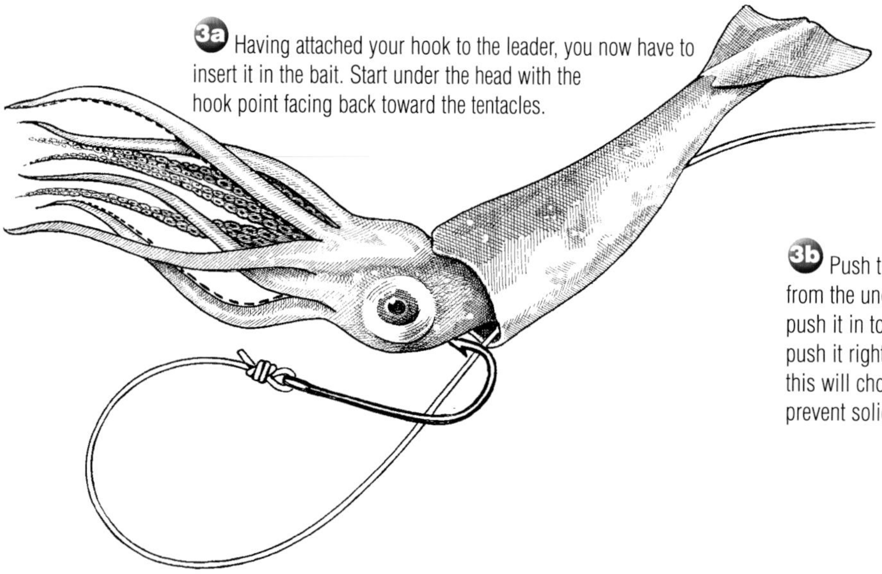

3b Push the hook point into, then out from the underside of the head, but don't push it in too deep. And, above all, don't push it right through the head because this will choke the hook and prevent solid hook-ups.

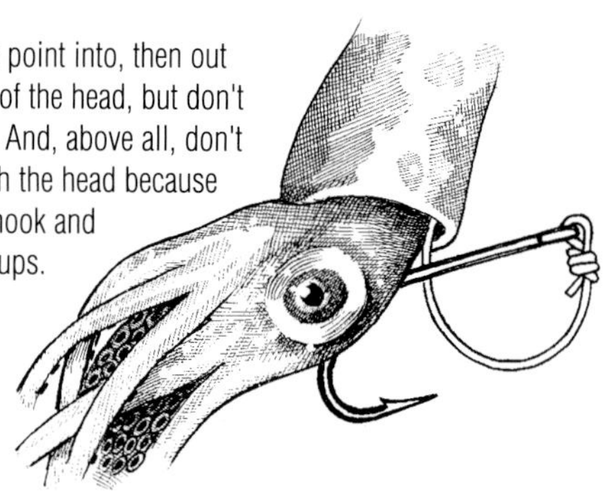

4 Take the remaining half of your galvanised wire and push it straight through the underside of the squid about halfway between the tip of the tail and where the leader emerges from the belly.

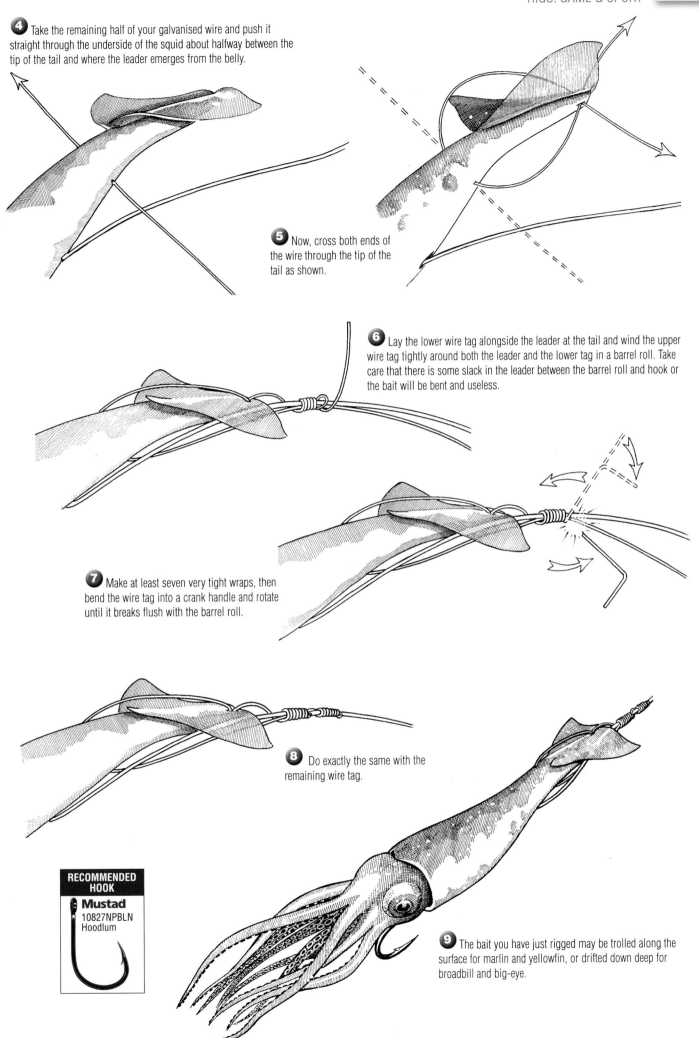

5 Now, cross both ends of the wire through the tip of the tail as shown.

6 Lay the lower wire tag alongside the leader at the tail and wind the upper wire tag tightly around both the leader and the lower tag in a barrel roll. Take care that there is some slack in the leader between the barrel roll and hook or the bait will be bent and useless.

7 Make at least seven very tight wraps, then bend the wire tag into a crank handle and rotate until it breaks flush with the barrel roll.

8 Do exactly the same with the remaining wire tag.

RECOMMENDED HOOK
Mustad
10827NPBLN
Hoodlum

9 The bait you have just rigged may be trolled along the surface for marlin and yellowfin, or drifted down deep for broadbill and big-eye.

PREPARING A BAITFISH FOR TROLLING

This troll bait rigging exercise makes use of either a heavy monofilament or a 49 strand wire leader. I used mullet for the baits in these illustrations but a variety of fish are suitable.

The materials used to rig these two baits include:

- A tube or needle to extend the leader through the fish.
- A stout needle and thread for stitching the gills and mouth.
- A suitable leader of heavy monofilament or 49 strand wire.
- A suitable size hook for the size of the fish you are using.
- A suitable size bean sinker for rigging a "swimming" bait.
- An shoemakers awl or similar puncturing device.
- A roll of .8 mm (.03 inch) galvanised tie wire for securing the tow point.

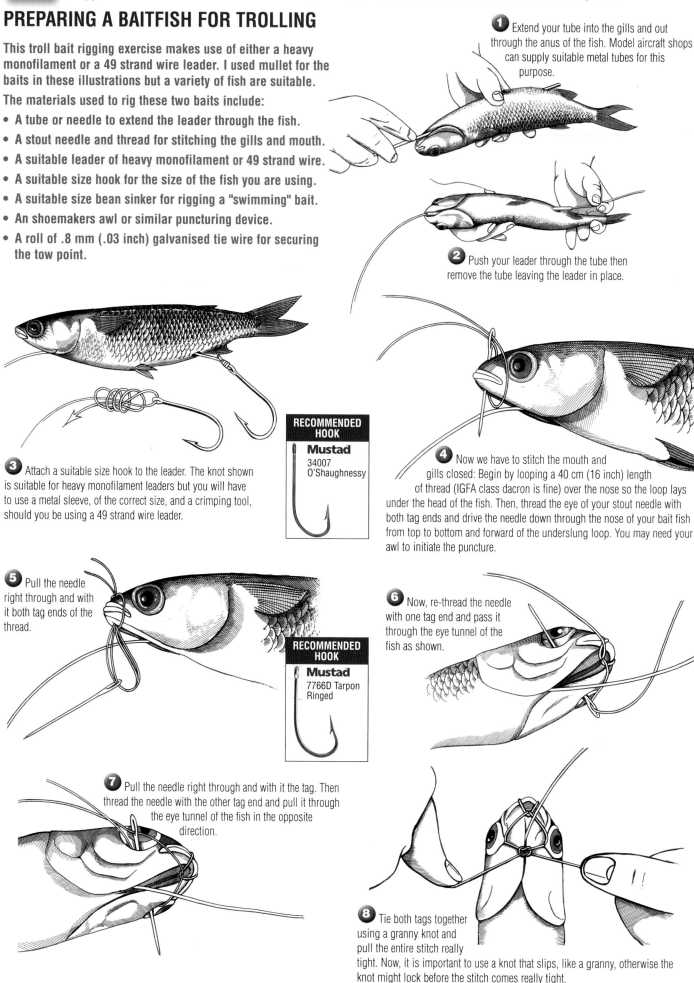

1 Extend your tube into the gills and out through the anus of the fish. Model aircraft shops can supply suitable metal tubes for this purpose.

2 Push your leader through the tube then remove the tube leaving the leader in place.

3 Attach a suitable size hook to the leader. The knot shown is suitable for heavy monofilament leaders but you will have to use a metal sleeve, of the correct size, and a crimping tool, should you be using a 49 strand wire leader.

RECOMMENDED HOOK
Mustad
34007
O'Shaughnessy

4 Now we have to stitch the mouth and gills closed: Begin by looping a 40 cm (16 inch) length of thread (IGFA class dacron is fine) over the nose so the loop lays under the head of the fish. Then, thread the eye of your stout needle with both tag ends and drive the needle down through the nose of your bait fish from top to bottom and forward of the underslung loop. You may need your awl to initiate the puncture.

5 Pull the needle right through and with it both tag ends of the thread.

RECOMMENDED HOOK
Mustad
7766D Tarpon Ringed

6 Now, re-thread the needle with one tag end and pass it through the eye tunnel of the fish as shown.

7 Pull the needle right through and with it the tag. Then thread the needle with the other tag end and pull it through the eye tunnel of the fish in the opposite direction.

8 Tie both tags together using a granny knot and pull the entire stitch really tight. Now, it is important to use a knot that slips, like a granny, otherwise the knot might lock before the stitch comes really tight.

At this point it is necessary to decide whether you are going to rig a "skip bait" on page 95, which will perform best when trolled fairly short from an outrigger, or whether you are going to rig a "swimming bait" as shown on page 96 which will perform in a similar manner to a large minnow type lure and which can be trolled right off the rod tip.

RIGGING A SKIP BAIT

The following instructions are for rigging a skip bait.

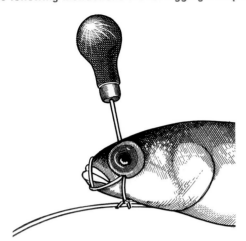

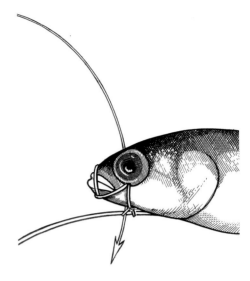

1 Puncture your bait right in the centre of the head, in the case of this mullet, that is right between the eyes. Then drive the awl right through so the point protrudes under the head.

2 Take about 40 cm (16 inches) of your .8 mm (.03 inch) galvanised tie wire and push one end down through the puncture you have made.

RECOMMENDED HOOK
Mustad
7766D Tarpon Ringed

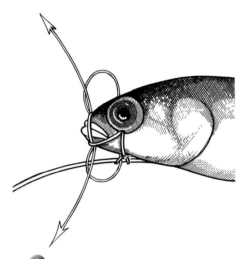

3 Now, push one end of the wire up through the first puncture you made, that's the one for the mouth stitch, and push the other end through in the other direction so they cross over within the forward puncture.

4 Bend the lower protruding wire forward so that it lays alongside the leader then wind the upper protruding wire tightly around both the leader and the lower wire.

RECOMMENDED HOOK
Mustad
34007 O'Shaughnessy

5 Having made a series of tight wraps with the upper wire, wrap the leader tightly with the protruding lower wire. Make the second set of wraps continue more or less flush with the first set. I have separated them so you can see more clearly what is happening.

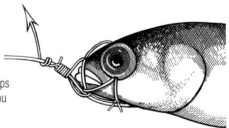

RECOMMENDED HOOK
Mustad
10827NPBLN Hoodlum

6 The completed bait should look something like this.

RIGGING A SWIM BAIT

The following instructions are for rigging a swim bait.

1 Use your awl to make a puncture central to the head of the fish only far enough back on the head to allow space for a suitable size bean sinker to be rigged under the head.

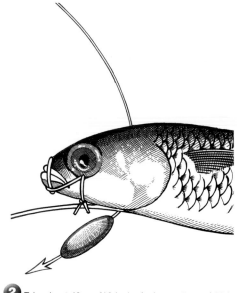

2 Take about 40 cm (16 inches) of your .8 mm (.03 inch) galvanised wire and push it right through the puncture made by your awl.

Then thread on your bean sinker which should be about the size shown in the diagram relative to the baitfish you are rigging.

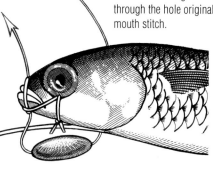

3 Push the tag of the wire back up through the hole originally made for the mouth stitch.

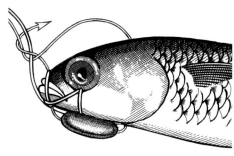

4 To form the towing bridle, raise the leader protruding from underneath the gills to a fairly sharp angle to the head of the fish.

Bend the wire protruding from the head forward, then sharply upward, to lay alongside the leader. Then commence a series of firm wraps around both leader and head wire with the wire protruding from the top of the fishes nose.

5 Having made a series of firm wraps around both leader and head wire, finish off by making another series of firm wraps around the leader with the tag of the protruding head wire.

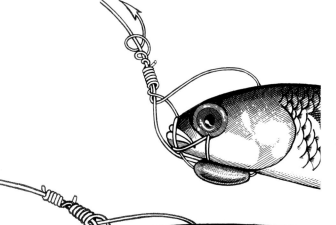

6 The result should look something like this with the fish secured on a bridle which—in combination with the sinker under the head—should make it swim in an attractive manner beneath the surface when towed directly from the rod tip.